Reach Your Potential
VIRGO

Teresa Moorey

Dedication

For Benjamin Elwyn 'Elf-friend', my youngest son, born while this book was in production

Orders: please contact Bookpoint Ltd, 39 Milton Park, Abingdon, Oxon OX14 4TD. Telephone: (44) 01235 400414, Fax: (44) 01235 400454. Lines are open from 9.00–6.00, Monday to Saturday, with a 24 hour message answering service. Email address: orders@bookpoint.co.uk

British Library Cataloguing in Publication Data
A catalogue record for this title is available from The British Library

ISBN 0 340 69714 8

First published 1998
Impression number   11   10   9   8   7   6   5   4   3   2
Year   2004   2003   2002   2001   2000   1999   1998

Copyright © 1998 Teresa Moorey

All rights reserved. No part of this publication may be reproduced or transmitted in any form or by any means, electronic or mechanical, including photocopy, recording, or any information storage and retrieval system, without permission in writing from the publisher or under licence from the Copyright Licensing Agency Limited. Further details of such licences (for reprographic reproduction) may be obtained from the Copyright Licensing Agency Limited, of 90 Tottenham Court Road, London W1P 9HE.

Typeset by Transet Limited, Coventry, England.
Printed in Great Britain for Hodder & Stoughton Educational, a division of Hodder Headline plc, 338 Euston Road, London NW1 3BH by Cox and Wyman, Reading, Berkshire.

Contents

INTRODUCTION	1
PERNICKETY, PERFECTIONIST OR PLAIN PERFECT – WHAT SORT OF VIRGO ARE YOU?	12

Chapter 1   THE ESSENTIAL VIRGO   17
- Not so neat and virginal   17
- Virgo body language   17
- Myths of the Virgin   18
- Element, Quality and Ruling Planet   19
- Private people   22
- A place for everything   23
- The know-it-all   25
- That critical factor   26
- The story of Baboushka   27
- The herb garden   29

Chapter 2   RELATIONSHIPS   32
- Virgoan sexuality   34
- Artemis and Orion   36
- Virgo woman in love   38
- Virgo man in love   39
- Gay Virgo   41
- Virgo love traps   41
- Virgo and marriage   43
- When love walks out – how Virgo copes   44

Chapter 3   ALL IN THE FAMILY   47
- Virgo mother   47
- Virgo father   49
- The Virgo child   50

	Virgo as siblings	53
	Virgo in the home	53
Chapter 4	FRIENDSHIPS AND THE SINGLE LIFE	56
	Virgo as a friend	56
	Virgo and the single life	58
Chapter 5	CAREER	60
	Traditional Virgo careers	61
	What to look for in your work	61
	Finger-in-the-dyke	62
	The critic	64
	The Virgo boss	65
	The Virgo employee	66
	When unemployment strikes	67
	Self-employment and other matters	68
Chapter 6	HEALTHY, WEALTHY – AND WISE?	70
	Health	70
	Money	72
	Wisdom	73
Chapter 7	STYLE AND LEISURE	75
	Your leisure	75
	Your style	77
Appendix 1	VIRGO COMBINED WITH MOON SIGN	80
Appendix 2	ZODIACAL COMPATIBILITY	88
	VIRGO COMPATIBILITIES	89
Appendix 3	TRADITIONAL ASSOCIATIONS AND TOTEM	102
FURTHER READING AND RESOURCES		106

Introduction

A PERSPECTIVE OF ASTROLOGY

Interest in the mystery and significance of the heavens is perhaps as old as humanity. If we can cast our imaginations back, to a time when there were no street lamps, televisions or even books, if we can picture how it must have been to have nothing to do through the deep nights of winter other than to sit and weave stories by the fire at the cave mouth, then we can come close to sensing how important the great dome of stars must have seemed in ancient times.

We are prone to believe that we are wiser today, having progressed beyond old superstitions. We know that all stars are like our Sun – giant nuclear reactors. We know that the planets are lumps of rock reflecting sunlight, they are not gods or demons. But how wise are we in truth? Our growing accumulation of facts brings us no closer to discovering the real meaning behind life. It may well be that our cave-dwelling ancestors knew better than us the meaning of holism. The study of astrology may be part of a journey towards a more holistic perception, taking us, as it does, through the fertile, and often uncharted realms of our own personality.

Until the seventeenth century astrology (which searches for the meaning of heavenly patterns) and astronomy (which seeks to clarify facts about the skies) were one, and it was the search for meanings, not facts that inspired the earliest investigations. Lunar phases have been found carved on bone and stone figures from as early as 15,000BCE (Before Common Era). Astrology then evolved through the civilisations of Mesopotamia and Greece, among others.

♍ VIRGO ♍

Through the 'dark ages' much astrological lore was preserved in Islamic countries, but in the fifteenth century astrology grew in popularity in the West. Queen Elizabeth I had her own personal astrologer, John Dee, and such fathers of modern astronomy as Kepler and Galileo served as court astrologers in Europe.

Astrology was taught at the University of Salamanca until 1776. What is rarely appreciated is that some of our greatest scientists, notably Newton and even Einstein, were led to their discoveries by intuition. Newton was a true mystic, and it was the search for meaning – the same motivation that inspired the Palaeolithic observer – that gave rise to some of our most brilliant advances. Indeed Newton is widely believed to have been an astrologer. The astronomer Halley, who discovered the famous comet, is reported to have criticised Newton for this, whereupon Sir Isaac replied 'I have studied it Sir, you have not!'

During the twentieth century astrology enjoyed a revival, and in 1948 The Faculty of Astrological Studies was founded, offering tuition of high quality and an examination system. The great psychologist Carl Jung was a supporter of astrology, and his work has expanded ideas about the mythic connections of the birth chart. Astrology is still eyed askance by many people, and there is not doubt that there is little purely scientific corroboration for astrology – the exception to this is the exhaustive statistical work undertaken by the Gauquelins. Michel Gauquelin was a French statistician whose research shows undeniable connection between professional prominence and the position of planets at birth. Now that the concept of a mechanical universe is being superseded, there is a greater chance that astrology and astronomy will reunite.

Anyone who consults a good astrologer comes away deeply impressed by the insight of the birth chart. Often it is possible to see very deeply into the personality and to be able to throw light on current dilemmas. It is noteworthy that even the most sceptical of people tend to know their Sun sign and the characteristics associated with it.

■ WHAT IS A BIRTH CHART?

Your birth chart is a map of the heavens drawn up for the time, date and place of your birth. An astrologer will prefer you to be as accurate as you can about the time of day, for that affects the sign

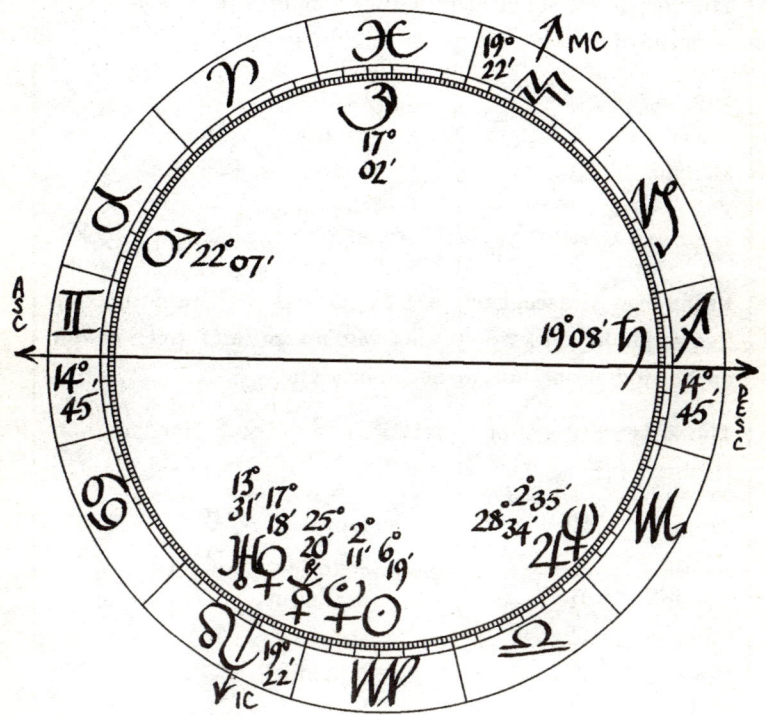

The birth chart of Michael Jackson
The Sun ☉ is conjunct Pluto ♀ in Virgo. Pluto gives Michael an intense drive to be the best he possibly can, in true Virgoan style.

rising on the eastern horizon. This 'rising sign' is very important to your personality. However, if you do not know your birth time a chart can still be compiled for you. There will be some details missing, but useful interpretations may still be made. It is far better for the astrologer to know that your birth time is in question than to operate from a position of false certainty. The birth chart for Michael Jackson (page 3) is a simplified chart. Additional factors would be entered on the chart and considered by an astrologer, such as angles (aspects) between the planets, and the houses.

> The **planets** are life principles, energy centres. To enable you to understand the birth chart, here are their glyphs:
>
> | Sun | ☉ | Jupiter | ♃ |
> |---|---|---|---|
> | Moon | ☽ | Saturn | ♄ |
> | Mercury | ☿ | Uranus | ♅ |
> | Venus | ♀ | Neptune | ♆ |
> | Mars | ♂ | Pluto | ♇ (P) |
>
> **Rising Sign** or **Ascendant** (**ASC**) is the way we have of meeting the world, our outward persona. **Midheaven** (**MC**) refers to our image, aspirations, how we like to be seen.
>
> The **signs** are modes of expression, ways of being. Here are their glyphs:
>
> | Aries | ♈ | Libra | ♎ |
> |---|---|---|---|
> | Taurus | ♉ | Scorpio | ♏ |
> | Gemini | ♊ | Sagittarius | ♐ |
> | Cancer | ♋ | Capricorn | ♑ |
> | Leo | ♌ | Aquarius | ♒ |
> | Virgo | ♍ | Pisces | ♓ |
>
> Using knowledge of the glyphs you can see that the Sun is in Virgo in our example birth chart (page 3).

♍ Introduction ♍

The birth chart shows each of the planets and the Moon in the astrological signs, and can be thought of as an 'energy map' of the different forces operating within the psyche. Thus the Sun sign (often called 'birth sign' or 'star sign') refers only to the position of the Sun. If the planets are in very different signs from the Sun sign, the interpretation will be greatly modified. Thus, if a person has Sun in Leo yet is somewhat introverted or quiet, this may be because the Moon was in reserved Capricorn when that person was born. Nonetheless, the Sun represents the light of consciousness, the integrating force, and most people recognise that they are typical of their Sun sign, although in some people it will be more noticeable than in others. The planets Mercury and Venus are very close to the Sun and often occupy the same sign, so intensifying the Sun-sign influence.

This book is written about your Sun sign, because the Sun sign serves as an accessible starting point for those wishing to learn about themselves through astrology. However, do not let your interest stop there. If you find anything helpful in comments and advice stemming from Sun sign alone, you will find your true birth chart even more revealing. The address of the Faculty of Astrological Studies appears in 'Further Reading and Resources' at the back of this book, and it is a good idea to approach them for a list of trained astrologers who can help you. Moon *phase* at birth (as distinct from Moon sign) is also very important. *The Moon and You for Beginners* (see 'Further Reading') explains this fascinating area clearly, and provides a simple chart for you to look up your Moon phase and learn what this means for your personality.

■ HOW DOES ASTROLOGY WORK?

We cannot explain astrology by the usual methods of cause and effect. In fact, there are many things we cannot explain. No one can define exactly what life is. We do not know exactly what electricity is, but we know how to use it. Few of us have any idea how a television set works, but we know how to turn it on. Although we are not able to explain astrology we are still able to use it, as any capable astrologer will demonstrate.

Jung discovered something called 'synchronicity'. This he defined as 'an acausal connecting principle'. Simply, this means that some events have a meaningful connection *other than cause and effect*. The planets do not cause us to do things, but their movements are synchronistic with our lives. The old dictum 'as above, so below' applies here. It is a mystery. We can't explain it, but that doesn't mean we should refuse to believe in it. A little boy on a visit to the circus saw an elephant for the first time and said 'There's no such thing'. We may laugh at the little boy, but how many of us respond to things we do not understand in this way?

The planetary positions in your birth chart are synchronistic with the time of your birth, when you took on separate existence, and they are synchronistic with your individuality in this life. They have much to say about you.

■ MYTH AND PSYCHOLOGY

The planets are named after the old gods and goddesses of Rome, which in turn link in with Greek and other pantheons. The planets represent 'life principles' – forces that drive the personality, and as such they can be termed 'archetypal'. This means that they are basic ideas, universal within human society and are also relevant in terms of the forces that, in some inexplicable way, inhabit the corners of the universe and inform the Earth and all human institutions. Thus the assertive energy that is represented by Mars means energetic action of all sorts – explosions and fires, wars,

♍ Introduction ♍

fierce debates and personal anger. Put briefly, here are the meanings of the planets:

- Mercury – intellect and communication
- Venus – love, unifying, relating
- Mars – assertion, energy, fighting spirit
- Jupiter – expansion, confidence, optimism
- Saturn – limitation, discipline
- Uranus – rebellion, independence
- Neptune – power to seek the ideal, sense the unseen
- Pluto – power to transform and evolve

These principles are modified according to the astrological sign they inhabit; thus Venus in Pisces may be gently loving, dreamy and self-sacrificing, while Venus in Aries will be demanding and adventurous in relationships. Thus the planets in signs form a complex psychological framework – and that is only part of the story of chart interpretation!

In the old mythologies these 'energies' or 'archetypes' or 'gods' were involved in classical dramas. An example is the story of Saturn and Uranus. Uranus is the rejecting father of Saturn, who later castrates and murders his father – thus innovative people reject reactionaries, who then murder them, so the revolutionary part of the personality is continually 'killed off' by the restrictive part. The exact positions and angles between the planets will indicate how this and other myths may come to life. In addition, the mere placement of planets by sign – and, of course, especially the Sun sign, call forth various myths as illustrations. The ancient myths are good yarns, but they are also inspired and vivid dramatisations of what may be going on repeatedly within your personality and that of your nearest and dearest. Myths are used by many modern psychologists and therapists in a tradition that has grown since Jung. We shall be using mythic themes to illustrate internal dynamics in this book.

♍ VIRGO ♍

SIGN	QUALITY	ELEMENT
Aries	Cardinal	Fire
Taurus	Fixed	Earth
Gemini	Mutable	Air
Cancer	Cardinal	Water
Leo	Fixed	Fire
Virgo	Mutable	Earth
Libra	Cardinal	Air
Scorpio	Fixed	Water
Sagittarius	Mutable	Fire
Capricorn	Cardinal	Earth
Aquarius	Fixed	Air
Pisces	Mutable	Water

■ THE SIGNS OF THE ZODIAC

There are twelve signs, and each of these belongs to an Element – Earth, Fire, Air or Water, and a Quality – Cardinal, Fixed or Mutable. The Cardinal signs are more geared to action, the Fixed tend to remain stable and rooted, whereas the Mutable signs are adaptable, changeable.

Jung defined four functions of consciousness – four different ways of perceiving the world – 'thinking', 'feeling', 'sensation' and 'intuition'. Thinking is the logical, evaluative approach that works in terms of the mind. Feeling is also evaluative, but this time in relation to culture and family needs. This is not the same as emotion, although 'feeling' people often process emotions more smoothly than other types. Jung saw 'feeling' as rational, too. 'Sensation' refers to the 'here and now', the five physical senses, while 'intuition' relates to the possible, to visions and hunches. Jung taught that we tend to have one function uppermost in consciousness, another one

♍ Introduction ♍

or maybe two secondary and another repressed or 'inferior', although we all possess each of these functions to some degree.

Jungian ideas are being refined and expanded, and they are incorporated into modern methods of personality testing, as in the Myers-Briggs test. If a prospective employer has recently given you such a test, it was to establish your talents and potential for the job. However, the basic four-fold division is still extremely useful, and I find that it is often of great help in assisting clients to understand themselves, and their partners, in greater depth – for we are all apt to assume that everyone processes information and applies it in the same way as we do. But they don't! It is worthy of mention that the important categories of 'introverted' and 'extraverted' were also identified by Jung. In astrology, Fire and Air signs seem to be extraverted, generally speaking, and Earth and Water introverted – and this has been borne out by the statistical research of the astrologer, Jeff Mayo. However, this doesn't mean that all feeling and sensation people are introverted and all intuitive and thinkers extraverted – this is definitely not the case, and calls for more detailed examination of the chart (e.g. lots of Fire and Water may mean an extravert feeling type).

Very broadly speaking we may link the Fire signs to intuition, Water to feeling, Earth to sensation and Air to thinking. Often thinking and feeling are drawn together and sensation and intuition are attracted, because they are opposites. This probably happens because we all seek to become more whole, but the process can be painful. The notion of the four functions, when understood, does help to throw light on some of the stumbling blocks we often encounter in relationships. However, some people just do not seem to fit. Also Fire doesn't always correspond to intuition, Water to feeling, etc. – it seems this is usually the case, but not all astrologers agree. Some link Fire with feeling, Water with intuition, and most agree that other chart factors are also important. As with all theories, this can be used to help, expand and clarify, not as a rigid system to impose definitions. We shall be learning more about these matters in relation to the Sun sign in following pages.

■ THE PRECESSION OF THE EQUINOXES

One criticism often levelled at astrology is that 'the stars have moved' and so the old signs are invalid. There is some truth in this, and it is due to a phenomenon called 'The Precession of the Equinoxes'. The beginning of the sign Aries occurs when the Sun is overhead at the equator, moving northwards. This is called the Spring Equinox, for now day and night are equal all over the globe, and the first point of Aries is called the 'equinoctial point'. Because the Earth not only turns on its axis but 'rocks' on it (imagine a giant knitting needle driven through the poles – the Earth spins on this, but the head of the needle also slowly describes a circle in space) the 'equinoctial point' has moved against the background of stars. Thus, when the Sun is overhead at the equator, entering Aries, it is no longer at the start of the constellation of Aries, where it occurred when the signs were named, but is now in the constellation of Pisces. The 'equinoctial point' is moving backwards into Aquarius, hence the idea of the dawning 'Aquarian age'.

So where does that leave astrology? Exactly in the same place, in actuality. For it all depends on how you think the constellations came to be named in the first place. Did our ancestors simply look up and see the shape of a Ram in the sky? Or did they – being much more intuitive and in tune with their surroundings than we are – feel sharply aware of the quality, the energies around at a certain time of the year, and *then* look skywards, translating what they sensed into a suitable starry symbol? This seems much more likely – and you have only to look at the star groups to see that it takes a fair bit of imagination to equate most of them with the figures they represent! The Precession of the Equinoxes does not affect astrological interpretation, for it is based upon observation and intuition, rather than 'animals in the sky'.

USING THIS BOOK

Reach Your Potential – Virgo explores your Sun sign and what this means in terms of your personality; the emphasis is on self-exploration. All the way through, hints are given to help you to begin to understand yourself better, ask questions about yourself and use what you have to maximum effect. This book will show you how to use positive Virgoan traits to your best advantage, and how to neutralise negative Virgoan traits. Don't forget that by reading it you are consenting, however obliquely, to the notion that you are connected in strange and mysterious ways to the web of the cosmos. What happens within you is part of a meaningful pattern that you can explore and become conscious of, thereby acquiring greater influence on the course of your life. Let this encourage you to ask further questions.

Some famous Virgos

Buddy Holly, Michael Jackson, Sophia Loren, Twiggy, Sean Connery, Jeremy Irons, Lauren Bacall, Prince Albert, Ingrid Bergman, Leonard Bernstein, Maurice Chevalier, Queen Elizabeth I, Greta Garbo, Goethe, D. H. Lawrence, Cardinal Richelieu, Peter Sellers, Edith Sitwell, Annie Kenney.

♍ VIRGO ♍

Pernickety, perfectionist or plain perfect – what sort of Virgo are you?

Here is a quiz to give an idea of how you are operating at the moment. Its tone is light-hearted, but the intent is serious and you may learn something about yourself. Don't think too hard about the answers, just pick the one that appeals to you most.

1. **You are waiting to be served in a restaurant, with a party of friends. The waiter is taking ages and everything seems quite sloppy, so you:**

   a) ☐ Get out your pen and notebook – you always have one with you – and make a note of *everything*, even counting the number of stains on the tablecloth. Then you check you have the telephone number of the Environmental Health Department. There will be some phone calls tomorrow!

   b) ☐ You sit in growing agitation, planning and refining a letter of complaint over and over again in your mind.

   c) ☐ You fight down the irresistible urge to go out into the kitchen and sort out the staff.

2. **You have been invited to a party. How do you view the prospect?**

   a) ☐ You really dislike parties. People so rarely have anything half-sensible to say. Inevitably you find yourself emptying ashtrays and watching people's elbows as they wobble, drunkenly, near full glasses.

   b) ☐ Parties aren't your favourite places to be. Often you form part of an earnest enclave in the kitchen. Sometimes you do the washing up. Usually you leave early.

   c) ☐ You like to see people enjoying themselves and you sometimes have a knees-up yourself. However, you also like to help the host/ess with food, clearing up, etc.

ᛏ Introduction ᛏ

3. **The gorgeous someone with the dreadful reputation has asked you out. Now what will you do?**

   a) ☐ Refuse – what's the point? You'd rather have an early night and a cup of cocoa.

   b) ☐ Say you'll think about it, and worry endlessly. Should you, shouldn't you, and how will you deal with it all?

   c) ☐ Say yes, and resolve to keep your cool, staying one jump ahead.

4. **A report you have produced, after burning several litres of midnight oil, is criticised by your immediate superior. How do you react?**

   a) ☐ You write a long letter to your boss, justifying your points.

   b) ☐ You go very reserved – you feel quite crushed and you wonder what else you're doing wrong.

   c) ☐ You argue your case coolly and efficiently – you know what you're talking about.

5. **You have suffered this same, crushing type of headache every day now for a fortnight. What do you do about it?**

   a) ☐ You read your medical textbooks (you have about a dozen) and you're sure its a brain tumour. You worry yourself sick and the headache is getting worse.

   b) ☐ This is called 'cluster headache'. You need more vitamin B6 and zinc – you're sure something in your medicine cupboard will help.

   c) ☐ You know your bodily responses. This is simply overwork. You decide to have a few early nights and more fresh air during the day, and you start by going to bed with a cool lavender compress on your forehead. Aah, that's better already!

♍ VIRGO ♍

6. **Which of the following sayings do you think best fits you, or do you like best/employ most often?**
   a) ☐ Excellence is my passion.
   b) ☐ A thing worth doing is worth doing well.
   c) ☐ Do your best, forget the rest.

7. **You come in late and find that your partner/flatmate has left the kitchen looking like the inside of a skip – and it's *his or her turn* to clear up and cook. Yes, this is the first time it's happened, but you just couldn't cope with a messpot permanently. What do you do?**
   a) ☐ Retire to your room, huffing and puffing and write down what you want to say in complaint. It covers two sides of A4, so you begin to wonder what you are going to do with it . . .
   b) ☐ Muttering and tutting, you set about clearing the mess.
   c) ☐ You decide that something must have upset your partner/flatmate, so you ask what's wrong. Both your curiosity and your compassion is aroused – and you don't want this happening again!

8. **You are rather late and stuck behind a long queue at the post office. The person at the front is asking stupid questions about postage rates. What do you do?**
   a) ☐ It's never happened to you, you have more sense than to run your life in that silly way, and you go only when you know there will be no crowds. (To tell the truth you do get rather tense at times, trying to keep tabs on your self-imposed schedules – and you'd better not spend too much time reading this book, as it's time to have your shower/clean your shoes/watch the daily news . . .)
   b) ☐ You cannot resist the temptation to pick up the relevant leaflet and present it to the questioner.
   c) ☐ You look at your list and decide to change your plans – you can come back later.

♍ Introduction ♍

9. You are walking through town when an old lady stops to let her dog foul the centre of the pavement. How do you react?

a) ❑ You quote her the relevant bylaw verbatim, demand to know her address, and inform the police.

b) ❑ You point out the error of her ways succinctly. Then you demand that she clears up the mess.

c) ❑ You observe that she is doddery, so you ask if she has proper control of her dog and offer to give her advice about 'pooper-scoopers'.

Now count up your score. What do you have most of – a's, b's or c's?

Mostly a's. At the moment the thoroughly pernickety side of Virgo has you in its prickly grip. You are determined to do everything properly, never get sidetracked into trivia, leave no stone unturned and sort out everyone. You worry a lot and it's no wonder! Can't you see you're attempting the impossible? Ease up and decide you will do certain things – the possible ones – well, and leave the rest. It will be far better for your health, and your efficiency.

Mostly b's. You are a fairly 'typical' Virgo. Although you know perfection is an impossibility you tend to aim for it. In general, you need to cultivate the pragmatist in you a little more. Ease up on your expectations of yourself and others, and rejoice in the wondrous perfection of your imperfections.

Mostly c's. It seems you're 'plain perfect'. Although you like to see things are done well, you do accept limitations. Yours is the art of the possible and you take into account the feelings of others. You are helpful, because you know how to be and you enjoy being practical and precise. You make everyone else feel inadequate, but we can't help being grateful.

♍ VIRGO ♍

If you found that in many cases none of the answers seemed anywhere near to fitting you, then it may be that you are an uncharacteristic Virgo. This may be because there are factors in your astrological chart that inhibit the expression of your Sun sign, or it may be because there is a preponderance of other signs, outweighing the Virgo part. Whatever the case may be, your Sun-sign potential needs to be realised. Perhaps you will find something to help ring a few bells in the following pages.

1 ♍ The essential Virgo

If you have great talents, industry will improve them: if you have but moderate abilities, industry will supply their deficiency

Sir Joshua Reynolds, *Discourses 2*

■ NOT SO NEAT AND VIRGINAL

Virgo means virgin, a fact known to those with even virtually no interest in astrology. Inevitably it gives rise to jokes, and the assumption that this sign is given to celibacy. In fact, nothing could be further from the truth. Second only to its opposite number, Pisces, Virgo is the most misunderstood sign of the zodiac. The second myth about Virgo concerns the extreme tidiness of the sign, and as we shall see, this is only partly true. The popular image of Virgo, enshrined in whitewashed sterility, clucking, scrubbing and picking bits of fluff off their clothing is very rarely encountered in real, live Virgos. However, like most myths both of these hide a truth.

■ VIRGO BODY LANGUAGE

This sign is rather low key, and very sensitive and responsive to cues from the environment. Because of this, Virgos tend to blend in with the background and have few outstanding mannerisms. Often there is a tendency to keep the head bent, and this can be noticeable even in extravert Virgos, whose dry wit keeps everyone giggling. It is possible to spot Virgos from their tendency to tilt the head to one side, sparrow-like, as if they are trying to make sure they hear everything – and probably they do. Sometimes, indeed, a Virgo will be unable to resist the temptation to straighten pictures and plump up cushions, and may have a go at cobwebs, too. However, such traits are more frequent with Virgo as a Rising Sign. Virgos rarely spread knees and elbows, and if their dress is not especially neat their posture often compensates. Their gestures are unassuming and when overwrought they may be driven to nail-nibbling and cuff-straightening. There may be a tendency to frown. Apart from this, others will need to be as observant as Virgos themselves to spot this modest sign.

MYTHS OF THE VIRGIN

We need to meet head on the image of Virgin, for it is entirely relevant to Virgo. The ancient meaning of the word has nothing to do with celibacy, for the requirement of virginity in women was a patriarchal development, designed to protect male inheritance and ownership. True 'virginity' has much more to do with self-possession, self-determination and the acknowledgement of the sacrality of sex, not in the sense of being forbidden or circumscribed, but rather as an expression of natural law and the power of the Goddess.

Virgo is named after the constellation of the Virgin, or Goddess of Justice, and legend tells how she retreated in disgust to the heavens when the Golden Age came to an end and humans no longer lived by her values. Older myths speak rather of the Corn Mother herself, Lady of the seasonal cycle and provider of fertility and bounty.

Such an image of the Feminine is very powerful, and it was reflected in ancient societies in the position of women themselves. Temple virgins were priestesses, and they were most certainly not celibate. Even the famed Vestal virgins were originally sexually active. Their 'virginity' consisted in their belonging to no man. They were 'self-possessed' in all senses of the word, and although they bestowed their sexual favours where they wished, or as the Goddess bade them, they retained their autonomy. This point is of prime importance to Virgo, whose deep psychological drive is 'self-possession' and the sifting of physical experience. Virgos wish to achieve order in their lives so that they may make better sense of the meaning of life and especially make sense of themselves. Every Virgo, however sensual – and many of the sign are very sexual creatures – seeks this sense of autonomy and proportion in the scheme of things, a wish to achieve internal orderliness and a proper place in the cosmos. We have departed a long way from the mop-and-bucket brigade!

The Corn Mother, or Great Mother, was rather more than a cornucopia of harvest goodies and fleshy pleasures. For not only was she the embodiment of fertility and growth, she also represented the inexorable culling of nature, the cutting of the corn, the sorting of the wheat from the chaff, the sacrifices, losses and natural selection that determined what was useful and able to support life, and what was to die. These dynamics are also evident in Virgo. Helpful and productive in the extreme, Virgo can also be critical and destructive. When this is exaggerated it is a distortion of what is a rightful process in the sign. Not everything is good enough and inferior produce must be relentlessly rejected in order that what is goodly may remain uncontaminated. Somewhere inside Virgo this process is operating continuously, weighing, measuring, sorting. It is a necessary psychological operation. These traits are just as evident in male Virgos, for they fit equally well with the masculine psyche.

■ ELEMENT, QUALITY AND RULING PLANET

We have seen that each of the signs of the zodiac belong to one of the Elements, Earth, Fire, Air or Water, and one of the Qualities, Cardinal, Fixed or Mutable. Virgo is Mutable Earth. Because of this

VIRGO

Virgo people display versatility and adaptability. You are able to come at a problem from various different angles and are resourceful in finding solutions. While you do not necessarily adhere to the status quo – remember, Virgo's quest is to discriminate and judge, and that means that what is found wanting may be rejected – you are generally extremely practical. The Earth influence orientates you to the useful and the realistic. No 'pie-in-the-sky' for Virgo – it has to be Momma's best apple pie, cooked to perfection from the highest quality fruit.

We have seen that the Element Earth has some things in common with what Jung called the Sensation function. This certainly doesn't mean the Earthy people are 'sensationalists', for the reverse is rather the case. It means that these people put their trust in what their five senses convey. It may be hard for more abstract types to understand this approach, but it is very grounding, concentrating and secure. Virgo moves in the domain of the tangible. The theoretical, the possible, the inspired may be hard for you Virgos to value unless you can perceive some practical use for it. Virgo may be interested in ideas, but you will always need to follow the thread of reasoned argument back down to solid ground, to see how much notions can be given actual expression and how they can serve in some fashion. Virgo's concern is the maintenance of existence in an orderly, sustainable structure. All things from religion down to agricultural technique may be entertained, but unless it can be shown to have a use, to increase efficiency and order and to provide sustenance it is rejected in the Virgoan thresher.

Virgo is the sixth sign of the zodiac, and the second Earth sign. We can visualise human experience beginning with Aries, the first sign of the Pioneer. This is followed by Taurus, sign of the Settler, the Farmer. Then comes Gemini, the Thinker and Communicator, and with Cancer we find a sense of Feeling and Family. After Cancer comes Leo, sign of the Sovereign, and so human society takes shape. Now we arrive at Virgo, the Reaper, the Keeper of Records and the Establisher of Order. In Virgo we see a sense of place in society and common good developing.

In the Northern Hemisphere Virgo precedes the Autumn Equinox. Now is the time of the first harvest, the hedgerow fruits and Keats' 'season of mists and mellow fruitfulness'. Harvesting, preserving, gathering, sorting are all themes of this time, as provision is made for the coming winter – and these are all Virgoan motifs. For those of you who live in the Southern Hemisphere it is the Spring Equinox that is presaged and you may prefer to think in terms of 'spring cleaning' to make way for the growing warmth of summer.

Each sign is said to have a 'Ruling Planet'. This means that there is a planet that has a special affinity with the sign, whose energies are most at home when expressed in terms of that sign. The Ruling Planet for Virgo is Mercury, shared with Gemini, but here we see Mercury in a different guise from the ethereal, unpredictable character of the Airy sign. Mercury, in addition to being the messenger of the Gods was also a psychopomp – a guider of the souls of the dead into the Underworld. Mercury was the only being who could do this and return unscathed. Here we have a much more serious face to the quicksilver god. In addition, Mercury was a god of fertility and was honoured in roadside ephigies with carved phallus, called hermeia (Hermes was the Greek equivalent to Mercury). Mercury is no simple deity, and in Virgo we see his serious and enigmatic face, for he has links with the mysteries of fertility and regeneration. Virgos who allowed themselves to be sidetracked into pernicketiness need to remind themselves of the wisdom of Mercury/Hermes and their essential mission, which is to be productive, selective, nurturing and guiding.

In fairly recent times a new planetoid has been discovered between the orbits of Saturn and Uranus. It is called Chiron, after the wounded healer of mythology, and some say this planet is the true ruler of Virgo. The jury is still out on this matter, and so for the moment we are better remaining with Mercury, who has, after all, many links with Virgoan characteristics.

■ PRIVATE PEOPLE

We have described Virgo as 'self-possessed' and perhaps we need to examine more closely what this actually means. While few Virgos are party animals, it is not typical of the sign to be loners, exactly. Virgos have too well-developed a sense of community and a wish to be a useful cog in the wheel than to isolate themselves in an ivory tower. Also this is a tactile sign, and while they do not like their body-space to be invaded without their approval, there is a strong need for physical contact in many Virgoans. They like to touch fabrics, surfaces, textures, although they may recoil in disapproval if something is inferior. Some also like to hug their friends – remember, this is an Earth sign. So much for the 'untouchable' reputation.

However, there *is* an untouchableness about Virgo, and like many things linked to this sign it is quite subtle. It has to do with self-respect and autonomy, and with the sense of oneself as a discrete entity. It is a deep need to preserve the integrity of the Self, to have a clear idea of where 'I' begin and 'you' end. Every one of you Virgos has a large 'private' sign blocking off your most intimate centre, and however much you relate and love there is a part of you that you never give, or to which you even allow entry. It's not because you won't, or because of some paranoid fear of being 'taken over'. It's rather because you can't – it's just the way you are. To be clear about oneself, to have a sense of boundaries and place is the starting point in developing ideas about everything – at least, that is the Virgoan method. All of the Earth signs struggle with the intangible and what we may call the 'spiritual', and if this isn't addressed in some form the life can become meaningless and repetitive. While Taurus may seek to solidify beliefs into practice – and even dogma – and Capricorn seeks mastery and structure, Virgo seeks a sense of Place. That place is here and you start with yourselves – where better?

Of course, this may not be expressed with a healthy conviction, especially if Virgo feels threatened or unsure – and this is when we see some of the characteristic touchiness and fussiness manifesting. A Virgo who has not felt able to create the sense of self as an inviolable core may be skittish as an unbroken colt, and may be literally celibate in order to try to achieve that inner purity. Others manifest the extreme tidiness of which the sign is often accused, while some place a barbed-wire fence of criticism around themselves. Some may become recluses. In some sense they do need to keep people out.

It is important for Virgos everywhere to honour, consciously, that need for privacy and personal autonomy. This does not mean keeping away from people or purposely concealing facts and motives; it means respecting one's own, inner core and fostering a relationship with the world around that is one's own, alone. It means a true self-respect, that we all seek in our diverse ways. Without this, Virgo does run the risk of becoming scratchy and critical, but with it there is no more confident and reassuring person alive, for Virgo is coming from a potent sense of inner poise.

A PLACE FOR EVERYTHING

Everyone who has even a smattering of astrological knowledge knows that Virgo is reputed to be tidy – but is this so? We may accept that Virgoan neatness is overrated, but surely there is no smoke without fire? This is true. The urge for order does figure in the life of every Virgo, and it is connected to our theme of self-possession, for how can you order and come to know yourself if all is chaos around you?

In the life of each Virgo there is almost invariably a special area of order. Yes, there is occasionally the sort of Virgo who can't leave the house in the morning if there is a mug or book out of place, and who suffers insomnia if their slippers are not arranged neatly at the foot of the bed, but these are a rarity. I have known several Virgos who have lived in virtual squalor, displaying an Earth-sign realism when it comes to the material world – well, it's just dirt, and if I clean it up today I'll have to do it again next week. I have also known more than one Virgo whose personal hygiene was less than exemplary – Earth women all, and what's a little fresh sweat among pragmatists? However, on closer scrutiny, an area of supreme excellence can be uncovered. This might be financial records, kept perfectly in red and black, and leaving not a penny unaccounted for. It might mean especially neat cupboards, in a house that is like the inside of a skip, so that Virgo can put his or her hands on socks and underwear in the dark – it all adds to the efficiency. Or, on close inspection, behind piles of magazine, knitting, old letters and half-eaten packets of biscuits, you may discern that the books in the bookcase are in alphabetical order.

In this way each Virgo translates an inner impulse to order into physical reality. Unless it gets out of hand it's a very good thing. And if you are one of the compulsive types of Virgo – the sort who has to take a mouthful from each side of the plate in turn so the perfection of the meal isn't disrupted by the coarse necessity of feeding your face – do ask yourself what you really wish to preserve. It certainly isn't the purity of the potatoes and cabbage. Redirect your considerable talents before the next migraine arrives.

■ THE KNOW-IT-ALL

This is an exemplary sign, with perhaps a few unimportant failings, but there are far worse things than a little fussiness and criticism, are there not? After all, Virgo is methodical, circumspect, efficient, often tirelessly helpful and resourcefully creative. Virgo can create an environment of reassuring stability and quiet charm, and often achieves far more, far better, in a day than the more showy signs achieve in a week. There is little that Virgo cannot manage with a little application – and this sign rarely lacks that. Virgo is often as sensitive to beauty as Pisces, as charming as Libra, as enterprising as Aries, as entertaining as Gemini and as philosophically deep as Sagittarius. With all this, surely one can put up with some muted nagging and curtain twitching now and again?

Yes, to be sure one can, but you Virgos have rather more up your perfectly pressed sleeve than that, and this sign that hides its brilliant light under a very large bushel is concealing some destructive potential in the same place. Living with a Virgo can be rewarding, reassuring and entertaining – it can also leave others feeling drained and quite useless. This is not because you will undermine them with criticism, for that is easily dealt with, if they develop the hide of a rhino and have a few criticisms of their own. You will be so preoccupied with defending yourself and repairing the fault that you will get off their back, at least temporarily. It is rather Virgoan kindness which is the real killer.

Being perfect, capable, knowing and helpful at every turn can be a most destructive form of oneupmanship that can leave the object of Virgoan solicitude with nothing, not even the opportunity to complain. Of course, such a Virgo is motivated by the deepest of inner insecurities – with a fear of being secretly incapable so that the only way he or she can possibly come close to feeling 'okay' is to annihilate the capabilities of everyone near, but so subtly that Virgo can be effectively confronted only by someone with the guts to appear selfish, ungrateful and aggressive in order to protect his or her own boundaries. Not easy. Anyone who said Virgo was self-effacing and harmless had best think again.

Some Virgos are quite excessive in their 'perfection'. They are an exaggeration of the potential that exists to make others feel small and incompetent. Others may rest assured that if their Virgo makes them feel like that, then that is how Virgo is feeling, deep inside. And if you recognise yourself, however diluted, here, then perhaps you need to ask yourself why it is you feel you have so little that you must rob everyone of what *they* have. In truth you are departing miles from that true Virgoan self-sufficiency into leaching the self-respect of everyone else. You owe yourself something better. Put your energies to positive use. Come into your own power and leave others to theirs.

■ THAT CRITICAL FACTOR

One of the primary Virgoan assets is the ability to criticise. Virgos often have laser-sharp brains that reach into the cracks of any construct. Any new project can be improved only by exposure to the X-ray eyes of a positive and discriminating Virgo. Naturally, however, this faculty can be hard to take, and sometimes it can be used destructively. Like an army of soldier ants, Virgo can march over one's pet crops and raze everything to the ground. Astrology is often a target, and many Virgos are at great pains to explain exactly, with examples, lists and details, why they are not in the least like their Sun sign. QED.

Virgos, however, may be deeply hurt by criticism and may fail to see their own failings – apparently. However, the truth of the matter is that Virgo is probably her or his own worst critic, and after all that

The essential Virgo

inward shredding it is just too much to take if others add their voices to all those inside Virgo's worried head that say 'That bit isn't quite right, you never do anything properly, you've made a mess again'. That might be really hard to believe when Virgo has done an A1 job, but it is so. Others shouldn't criticise a Virgo, unless they slice it thinly and sandwich it between thick compliments. Virgos can't always take it and they're deeply hurt. They should be left to their own standards – they're far higher than anyone else's!

If you are a Virgo, recognise that your ability to criticise is a fine scalpel that you have to use with the responsibility of a surgeon. This faculty is needed and you may be depended on to use it. Always use it wisely and positively, and try to be aware that others may be hurt by it. It is possible to have truth and comfort, with a bit of tact, and you will be respected all the more if you take into account other people's feelings. Don't turn your criticisms on yourself, for it is a form of internal suicide. Use them to improve yourself, not demolish what you have done, which is likely to be excellent.

The story of Baboushka

A Russian Christmas story tells of the industry of Baboushka. All the people in her village were excited by the rumours of a great event. A bright star was seen, nightly, in the sky and there were tales of a procession heading towards their small settlement. Baboushka had no time for all the whispering – she had too much work to do, cooking and scrubbing and keeping her cottage spick and span.

She did not see the line of lights on the horizon, for she had her head bent over her tub, but when there was a knock at her door she jumped up. To her amazement there were three kings on her step with their attendants. 'Yours is the best house in the village,' they said. 'Do you have a place for our masters to sleep?'

♍ VIRGO ♍

Baboushka threw wide her door and scurried to her kitchen. 'Welcome, welcome,' she said, as she placed homemade pies and bread, yogurts, cheeses, borsch and wine before her grateful guests. 'Come with us,' they said, after they had satisfied their hunger. 'We follow a star to the new-born King. Bring him a gift as we do – your excellent homemade wine will be perfect.'

'Oh, that isn't fit for a baby,' cried Baboushka, laughing and blushing. Then she looked sad. 'I have a cupboard full of toys,' she said. 'They belonged to my own little son, who died when he was tiny.'

'Then come with us tonight, when the star shines again,' said the kings. 'Our new baby king can be yours too.'

'I'll think about it,' said Baboushka, and through the long hours while they slept she cleared up, cleaned up and made everything spotless once more. She baked more pies, bottled more wine and at last fell into an exhausted sleep. Soon night had fallen again and the kings said to Baboushka 'Are you ready?' 'No, no, not quite,' said Baboushka. 'I'll have to catch you up – there's still so much to do here.' The kings sadly left her, and Baboushka cooked and cleaned again. Then she opened the toy cupboard, intending to pack. My, how dusty all those toys were! They weren't fit for any baby, let alone a little king. She would have to give them a good clean . . . On and on, into the night, she polished and scrubbed until all the toys gleamed. as she was finishing, the cockerel crowed in the nearby farm. 'I'll be on my way, now,' thought Baboushka, 'but I'm so tired . . . perhaps just forty winks before I set off.'

When she awoke, night had fallen again but there was no star to be seen. Baboushka quickly grabbed the bag of toys, locked the door behind her and hurried off into the night – but she could find no sign of the three kings. Through towns and villages she journeyed, asking after the procession, but always she was too far behind. At last, she

> came to Bethlehem, and the innkeeper showed her the stable where the holy family had slept. 'Was there really a baby here?' asked Baboushka. 'Yes, a special baby indeed,' came the reply. 'The shepherds came as soon as the angels told them, the kings came when they saw the star. They told me about you, but I am sorry, you are too late. The family have gone to find safety in Egypt. But you may sleep here the night, for this is where the Saviour of the World was born.'
>
> But Baboushka could not rest, and legend tells that she does not rest to this day. On and on she travels, looking for Baby Jesus. At Christmas time she leaves her toys by the beds of sleeping children, but her bag never empties. She searches and searches for the Christ Child, and some say she will do so until the end of time.

Here we have a poignant story of goodness and industry that were taken too far, depriving she who practised them of her rightful rewards. Of course, children all over the world benefit from Baboushka's never-failing generosity – but what about Baboushka herself? Baboushka is a typically Virgoan figure who went above and beyond the call of duty. If you see yourself here, then ease up, before it is too late. Stop working before it eats up all your time for joy. Enjoy the delights that all your 'hot pies' and 'best pickles', that your sparkling home and your carefully preserved toys have earned you. Rest on your laurels, open your eyes to that bright star and open your heart to a time of recreation.

THE HERB GARDEN

We have spoken much about Virgoan discrimination, orderliness and talent for criticism, and while all these are praiseworthy and very positive traits, they are not always heartwarming. However, this is far from being the full story of Virgo. If you remember, we linked the sign of Virgo to the Earth Mother, the Great Goddess herself. Virgo has tremendous nurturing qualities. Productive, sincere and caring, this sign is usually 'growing' something, from delicious homegrown herbs and vegetables (many Virgos have green fingers) through fine sculpture and financial empires to the store of knowledge in themselves and other. These people are great teachers. They are as full of information as any Gemini but they usually have more precise ideas as to its application. With Virgo nothing is wasted. Virgos are not so much 'perfectionists', for perfection is unrealistic – they are pragmatists. The unwanted is turned into a compost and nourishes the soil.

Perhaps we can turn away from the notion of sweeping and sorting and place our typical Virgo in a metaphorical herb garden. Herbs are useful for cooking and medicine, they are of ancient stock, unweakened by hybridisation, and although modest they are fragrant and often very beautiful. Herbs speak of the power of the earth in companion with human effort. Virgos may like to tend the herbs, feeling the soft soil between their fingers, they may pluck them for the cooking pot or the infusion, they may brush by them, for the sheer joy of their scent, while they read philosophy or ponder some intellectual conundrum, or they may paint them on canvas, for their beauty. One thing Virgo will not do, at least not for very long, is sit in the garden and dream – this is a sign that prefers reality, on the whole, because you can *do* something with it. Of course, our 'herbs' may be computer programs, balance sheets, creative writing, healing, teaching, organising – in short, any of the multitude of talents possessed by Virgos. Cultivate them, in keeping with natural balance, and do not forget simply to enjoy.

■ PRACTICE AND CHANGE ■

- Remember the story of Baboushka. Do not allow an obsession with perfection to blind you to true opportunity. Never forget, work, rest and play in equal measure.
- The ability to make intelligent criticism is a talent you have that must not be abused. Remember to remark also on the positive aspects. And do not criticise yourself beyond what is healthy. Remember to give yourself pats on the back.
- Self-possession is your birthright. If you feel invaded, perturbed or 'run ragged' then you need to create space for yourself and peace in your soul to retrieve your autonomy. Take walks in the country to reaffirm your contact with the natural world.
- There is no doubt that you know a great deal. You do not need to know it all. Give other people the space to be experts in their fields. Goodness knows you must have enough work to do!
- Nature and nurture are both your areas. You are extremely creative and will feel gratified if you have something wholesome and productive to show for your efforts. Use your energies wisely – tidying and sorting will not fulfil you.
- You are a great one for helping others, but you may find it very hard to let them help you. Try to ease up on this. Everyone is gratified by the knowledge that they have lent a helping hand, and it will leave you free to do something of your choice. Use that choice creatively.

2 ♍ Relationships

Familiar acts are beautiful through love

Shelley, *Prometheus Unbound*

Virgo is an enigmatic sign, and nowhere is this more noticeable than in relationships. Deep inside the pragmatist there's a whimsical romantic. Virgo may be at great pains to conceal this, but in your more relaxed moments it peeps out. An appreciative lover can coax Virgo into passion and enchantment, but this may take time and a lot of patience. Earth signs are slow to warm up, and diffident Virgo may be the slowest.

This sign rarely falls in love easily, although you may readily respond sexually – but that is another story. Virgos do not expect perfection in a partner – after all, you are realists and we all know that no human is perfect. However, you do like to know all the faults of your dearly beloved, and it takes time to observe and weigh. This can be very difficult to cope with, and sensitive souls may be convinced that passion has died as Virgo counts the blackheads on their nose, and informs them of the number – probably with recommendations for the skin treatments. However, such things do not affect Virgo's feelings one jot. It's a purely practical matter, and after all, how can you possibly take effective action against blackheads or anything else if you don't know exactly what you are up against?

Virgo's feelings run deep, but they are rarely obvious or easily aroused. It takes more than physical beauty to stir this measured heartbeat. Virgos like to know there is mental rapport as well as physical, and, like Capricorn, you often like to establish that the relationship will support your work, or at least pose no threat to it. Public displays of emotion – or even private ones – can be very embarrassing for some Virgos. In short, you can feel deeply disturbed by anything that you cannot control or fix, and so you may apparently switch off, just when you might be expected to respond with feeling. To Virgo 'truly, madly, deeply' is more comfortably replaced by 'truly, sensibly, sincerely'.

This may make Virgo sound a little boring, and occasionally Virgos bear out this impression. However, one needs to look below this surface image. Still waters run deep, and Virgo is aware that one is never so vulnerable as when in love. It is all well and good for the more superficial and careless to cast themselves into love's maelstrom, but you know that despite your resilience you will not easily repair sails torn ragged by storms of passion. Yes, you can go somewhat cold if you feel betrayed, criticised or threatened – and emotional demands can mean a threat. Yes, in love you do sometimes seem to lack enthusiasm. However, deep within, every Virgo yearns for wild delight, romance and ardour.

You need a partner who is spontaneous, playful, fervent and adventurous – and you need all this served up in small portions, so you aren't overwhelmed, have time to adjust and cautiously respond. Of course, this is asking a lot, and others may need to be a little clairvoyant to sense what is in the soul of Virgo and get the balance right. It is worth working on, however. The reward can be devotion, generosity, gentleness, tireless help and a delicate romanticism. Last but not least, they will benefit from the superb, practised sensuality of an aroused and trusting Virgo. It could be well worth it!

■ VIRGOAN SEXUALITY

Sexually, Virgo has some surprises, for this is the sign of the Great Harlot, the Sacred Whore. These images come down to us from a time when sex was both sacred and profane, when it embodied the raw power of nature and was synonymous with fertility and pleasure. Although in very ancient times the sexual act may have been seen as a participation in the mysteries of the Goddess, an almost magical act, yet it was probably not set deeply in an emotional context, and certainly not regarded in the moral fashion that is adopted today. All these considerations have a bearing on the ambiguous approach that Virgos may have to their sexuality. Because of the social context Virgos can be bothered by morals and mores and may fuss with manuals and sex guides. However, let us remind ourselves once more that this is an Earth sign, and sex, as a natural bodily function, can come very easily to them.

Most of us, in our youth, spent time secretly thumbing through sex manuals – and Virgo is certainly no exception to this. Virgo likes chapter and verse, and anything that describes 'how to' has an irresistible attraction for them. In addition, this is rarely a confident sign. The result may be a nervous lover, who moves to a set formula. Emotionally, Virgo may be totally absent and the lover may feel more like a vacuum cleaner than an object of desire.

However, Virgos who move beyond this and who acquire the assurance to express their Earthiness are a very different matter. Here we have a lover who is prepared to explore every corner of pleasure. In bed you can be a very considerate partner, for you are both skilful and sensitive to response. Once unleashed yours is a very sensual sign indeed. Nothing is necessarily taboo, because, when all is said and done, sex is sex. Virgo may thrive on kinky ideas and be very quickly aroused by the correct stimulus. It is rarely necessary to appeal to your imagination, for the 'here and now' is what counts, and while many Virgos do relish pornography and have some rather individual tastes, no mythical scenario is playing behind that cool gaze.

This sign has a reputation for prudery that is mostly quite unjustified. A Virgo who has taken the trouble to overcome prejudices is a most accepting character. However, occasionally Virgo can have hang ups. You may 'get off' on the feeling that you are being a 'naughty boy or girl' and while you may be prepared to indulge your own little preferences, you may become a little tight-lipped if your lover whispers his or her own fantasies about rubber gloves and galoshes. When it comes to the rest of the world you may just wax a trifle moralistic on occasion – but these tendencies in Virgo have been greatly overemphasised.

Female Virgos often take sex and the loss of their virginity very seriously – perhaps they are haunted by the traditional 'maiden aunt' image, and many seek sexual experience as early as possible rather than run the risk of being saddled with this. Virgo ladies can be very seductive, their tantalising untouchability mixed with subtle, but unmistakable hints of sexual know-how. Their hearts rarely rule their heads, and some may be capable of exploitation. If your feelings are not engaged it is so easy to get your own way, and Virgo, ever the pragmatist, is not slow to spot the possible advantages and to employ the correct skills. At heart, however, this lady is the Earth Mother. She longs to find a man who can supply her with security, not make too many inroads upon her privacy, and allow her the time she needs to blossom. Then she becomes the most warm, tender, caring and exciting partner any man can imagine – and that's not once upon a time in the bordello, it's every night.

Mr Virgo can be a very nervous adolescent and many Virgoan males fight shy of the entire sex thing until maturity has at least lent them some dignity. As Virgo is an unconvincing boaster it may be hell in the locker room for this adolescent. Later on, however, Virgo comes into his own. That Earth-sign realism and comfort with the body ensures that male Virgos leave all the wannabee studs far behind, as they quietly walk off with the stunning blonde everyone else has been drooling over. Not that this man is ever a sucker for a pretty face – mind has to catch up with matter if this guy is ever to catch fire. Then it will be a steady smoulder. Mr Virgo is neither one for damp fizzles nor flashes in the pan. Quiet he may be, but often unforgettable.

Many Virgos, it's true, do have a little bother getting their hearts and their genitals to work in tandem. You may sometimes fear that sex mixed with emotion is just asking for trouble – how can you keep the floodgates closed on all of that? It may be hard for you to let go with the person you love, and some Virgos become somewhat promiscuous, seemingly adopting the belief that there is safety in numbers. However, with a little understanding and a lot of time, Virgo can find that the most comfortable, safest and most pleasurable sexual experience is found in a committed and trusting relationship.

Artemis and Orion

Artemis, the maiden goddess, is a supremely Virgoan figure. There are many tales of how she savagely guarded her privacy, keeping the company of wild beasts in the forest – a perfect Virgoan blend of the primitive and the restrained. Although called 'maiden' we have already seen that such terms do not necessarily imply technical virginity, and Artemis, for all her self-possession, was capable of love. One story tells of her passion for Orion, most beautiful of the race of giants, and a superb huntsman himself. Her brother, Apollo, was jealous of their love and wishful of protecting his sister's reputation for purity – a Virgoan theme!

♍ Relationships ♍

> Apollo knew that Artemis could never resist a temptation to show off her skill with the bow. How she prided herself on her accuracy and control! When she drew back the string every nerve and fibre in her body quivered with concentration and determination to strike home. So as she stood on the sea shore, one day, waiting for Orion to return from his swim, Apollo came up to her and challenged her to send an arrow into a piece of wood they could just see, bobbing on the top of the waves, far out to sea.
>
> 'You'll never hit that,' mocked Apollo. 'Why, it looks no more than a speck from here. I bet your arrow falls wide.'
>
> 'We shall see,' said the goddess, tight lipped. She drew back the string, slowly and carefully, paused for a second and let fly the arrow. It sang out, over the waves and buried itself in the block of wood. But wood does not cry out when hit. Nor does it thresh about and slowly submerge under the weight of an arrow. Artemis turned pale as death as she realised what she had done. For what she had pierced with her arrow had been the head of her lover, Orion, who was now lost to her forever beneath the waves. So overwhelming had been her wish to prove her skill that she had killed the man she loved.

This sad story has a message for Virgo. Virgos, in their quest for precision, may kill much in the way of feeling. Sometimes it can be so important for Virgos to prove that they are right, or to get at the truth that they destroy what is of true value. A simple example of this appeared at the start of the chapter – why tell someone you love about their spots? Because they're there, Virgo may reply. Well, so what? To Virgo the arrow of critical assessment must find its mark, and sometimes it may bury itself deep in the heart of a loved one who just can't believe that there can be any feeling in someone who values precision for its own sake and neglects sensitivity. Virgoan relationships do sometimes founder on this. If you are a

Virgo, remember to ask yourself how much is worth sacrificing for 'the facts'. Remember how sensitive you are – do you really want to kill the thing you love to prove a point? Or would you not rather use that superb discrimination to identify just the right thing to say and do to enrich your relationship?

■ VIRGO WOMAN IN LOVE

This isn't often a lady who will fall 'in love with love'. Often it seems to her that the world would run much better without it – indeed, she probably can't understand it, until it hits her. The 'untouchable' quality in Virgo is very much in evidence in the females of the sign. Many things can feel almost like rape to Virgo – it isn't just a physical matter. Anyone or anything that makes assaults on her privacy or independence is experienced as violating. Anyone involved with a Virgo needs to have a highly developed awareness of how she defines her personal boundaries. Virgo, for her part, needs to try to be sure, first, that she has been clear about her need for space, and second that she is being reasonable – for compromises sometimes have to be made in the cause of relationships, as adaptable Virgo will understand. A Virgo who is sure of herself and her ability to control her environment has that subtle air of sexual awareness, poise and seductiveness that are the property of this mutable Earth sign alone.

When Ms Virgo does fall in love, she may do so deeply and completely. Not in a hurry to give her heart, she may not be able readily to retrieve it, and she can behave like a true heroine for whom the world is 'well lost for love'. There are Virgos who never really love, and these may be capable of using sex to their own ends – and that includes in marriage. However, life to such Virgos is eternally empty and meaningless. The Virgo who has found love, on the other hand, is mistress of all the erotic arts. Subtle, tantalising yet satisfying, reliable yet mysterious, nurturing, teasing, remote yet deliciously available, she is all woman in one package. Yes, she will notice that her lover didn't put the top on the toothpaste. She will want to know how much he earns and why he wasn't promoted last year, but she doesn't expect him to be perfect – she just wants to catalogue his imperfections. She's worth it. Who said living with a goddess was a pushover?

■ VIRGO MAN IN LOVE

Women who live for flamboyant declarations and dramatic gestures will have gathered by now that Mr Virgo isn't their guy. Mr Virgo is usually low key. He can't readily unleash his emotions and he's awful at faking – although Virgo isn't above the occasional resourceful lie; acting in situations such as this is rarely his talent. If his lover makes demands he will withdraw disdainfully, and if she decides that he's her rock, she'll find herself on shifting sand – he doesn't like to think that she expects too much of him or wants to draw him into too intimate a situation too quickly, because he usually underestimates his ability to 'deliver'. He's no one's idea of the romantic hero and he hardly lives up to the traditional image of the male as protector and provider. So maybe we should give this man a wide berth and head *en masse* for the Capricorns and Leos? No way. To miss Mr Virgo is to pass up on a treasure, although this may not be obvious at first.

If a woman earns his trust, coaxes out his sexual side and shows that she respects his inner privacy, Mr Virgo can hardly be improved upon as a mate. He is a devoted helper, a patient listener and he doesn't expect her to feed his ego. He will give her his advice and attention, and respond with painstaking, practical help. He's a real

Mr Fixit. His shoulder is there to cry on if her best friend lets her down (and he won't mind *very* much, even if it is his best shirt), and he has an answer to everything from a collapsed soufflé to a collapsed roof. The great thing about Mr Virgo is that he will almost always listen. Of course, she may not always like what he says in response, but at least she'll be dealing with the truth, not moonshine or bombast.

This is a fairly serious guy, but Virgo is full of surprises and some even will live dangerously for love. One Virgo man I know conducted an affair with his nextdoor neighbour, and allowed himself to be carted around in the boot of her car, for purposes of concealment. The emotional tension got too much, and on her wedding anniversary his lover announced to him, over the garden fence, that she was going to tell her husband about their relationship, so perhaps he had better tell his wife, because Harry was sure to do so if he didn't. Cool, eh? No threats or histrionics, just a simple *fait accompli*. This lady certainly knew her Virgo! What could he do? Being a realist it was obvious that no lies or manipulations were going to make any difference – there was no way out but to come clean. To the credit of his basic integrity and courage, that is exactly what this Virgo did, and after many difficult months he did set up home with his new lady. They are very happy, and have no regrets, but when he speaks about that time in his life it is in the tone of one who knows what it is like to live on top of the San Andreas fault. It isn't an experience he would care to repeat!

A woman whose taste is for the obvious or the flashy, or who simply wants to hang up her coat and her independence and have some strong man take charge of her life should accept that Mr Virgo is hardly for her. However, if she wants the love and respect of a man who knows what it means to be a partner, and who will allow her the same autonomy he requires himself, if she prizes quiet wit, kindness, wisdom and capability, then she has enough good taste to deserve Mr Virgo. He's a rare prize.

■ GAY VIRGO

It may be a type of hell for one of this sensitive and self-effacing sign to find he or she departs from the mainstream in a way that cannot be concealed, at least not completely, if he or she is to find satisfaction in love. Virgos may try very hard to convince even themselves that they are 'straight' and may embrace a conventional life of marriage and 2.4 children when it is the very last thing their hearts want. On the other hand, many Virgos will decide not to bother with relationships, if they are that troublesome, and just stay in the closet. Occasionally, gay Virgos may opt for promiscuity, which can be conducted in concealment, if you know where to go, rather than risk the commitment of an open partnership. As attitudes become more open help is more readily available. Of course, most Virgos just hate to be helped by others, but in this case you really do need help of some sort, even if it's just someone to talk to, both to adjust and to find companionship. This may be gruelling, for you are a very private person, but it brings undeniable rewards. None of us can function entirely on our own. Again it is about facing facts.

■ VIRGO LOVE TRAPS

'I'm not good enough'

Virgos expect an awful lot from themselves, and you are your own worst critics. In love relationships this can result in you making a virtual doormat of yourselves in order to save a relationship that is far better abandoned. Even love rarely blinds Virgo, but although this sign is a great cataloguer of shortcomings it does not necessarily reject on the basis of them. You do not so much expect perfection as like to know what you are dealing with. However, although it may be obvious to everyone else that what you are dealing with is selfishness, deceit and even violence, you Virgos may still believe that somewhere, somehow, it is of your making and if only you could Get It Right all would come good.

Now, of course, this is nonsense and you can't make a silk purse out of a sow's ear. Further than this, doormats belong on the floor and if you lie on the floor someone – everyone – will walk over you. Pisces, the sign most noted for self-sacrifice, is no match for Virgo when it comes to this sort of self-abasement. Any Virgo in this position needs to wake up to the fact that there are some things you just can't fix and this certainly isn't your fault. Get up, dust yourself off and say a firm 'Goodbye'. Ask yourself whether there isn't a type of pride tying you to this situation. Are you determined to prove there is nothing you can't make good? It's a mission impossible. Get real, and get back your self-respect. In a few years' time, when you look back on this situation, you will hardly recognise yourself.

'If at first you don't succeed . . . '

This 'love trap' is similar to the previous one. There is less self-abasement involved, but still an unwillingness to admit defeat. 'There must be some way to make this work,' Virgos may say to themselves, as habit and emotion draw them back yet again into a relationship that didn't work last time, or the time before, or the time before . . . The problem is that the more often you come back for a second, third, fourth try the easier it is to have another go. You are scooping out a rut for yourself to slide into time and again.

It is a tragedy that some relationships don't work, despite the best intentions of both concerned, and it is even worse when children and a shared home are the casualties. Despite the mutability of the sign Virgos are often highly resistant to change – although when change is inevitable they usually adapt extremely well. If you are in this sort of situation, it is rather like having to pull an aching tooth – painful, but much better when it's over. Take a deep breath and cut the ties for good. That way you have the hope of a bright future.

VIRGO AND MARRIAGE

Virgos do not usually rush into marriage, and there is a tiny kernel of truth in the idea that the sign is often happy being single. Not that there is any statistical support for a larger number of unmarried Virgos than any other sign. Rather it is the characteristics of the sign that make the single state valuable. In the first place there is autonomy and independence. No one to make demands, to invade privacy or to cause upheaval. In the second place there is the risk factor. This is a cautious sign, and the financial and other commitments entailed in marriage are not lost upon you. And then we have the beast of tidiness – not valued by every Virgo, it is true. However, it may be control rather than neatness that is the issue. This can be violated by someone with whom you share hearth and home.

This means that Virgos who do tie the knot are aware of the big step they are taking and they usually do so with a sense of responsibility. Because of this, they often do their very best to make marriage work. Of course, there are some who, in the event, find the intimacy too much, and certainly the responsibility of children is enough to send the occasional Virgo scurrying back to the bachelor pad (this includes females of the sign). However, married Virgos are among

♍ VIRGO ♍

the most loyal and devoted anyone could meet. Virgo knows the meaning of 'helpmeet'. Although you do need your own space, you are not a partner to compartmentalise shopping, cooking, cleaning and working, unless it is for the most practical of reasons. Virgos are good at teamwork and you like to build a comfortable nest, a bastion against life's variables. Virgo is not an easily understood sign, and you do not hastily form relationships. Having found understanding, companionship, loving support and good sex, Virgo gives a great deal and does not abandon ship in a hurry.

■ WHEN LOVE WALKS OUT – HOW VIRGO COPES

This is the sign of the 'coper' and Virgo will often move, apparently seamlessly, from what seemed a good and close relationship back into solitary splendour. On looking a little more closely, however, there may be signs that all is not well. Of course, it may have been that the Virgoan heart was never touched. On the other hand, some compulsive sorting and cleaning, a rather bustling and ostentatious (for Virgo) self-sufficiency and frequent visits to the doctor may tell another story. Most classic of all is the tendency for Virgos to throw themselves twenty-four hours a day into work. Virgos can be left deeply shaken by the end of a love affair – so much so that they actually become ill. Often this takes the form of a string of small maladies, from 'flu to stomach ache. Occasionally, it can signal the onset of something more serious.

If you have just lost a loved one, believe me it will do you no good whatsoever to tell yourself that you aren't hurt, that it doesn't matter and that you can carry on regardless – you can't, and if you try, your body may let you down. Your heart knows when it is broken even if your head persists in denying it. Of course, you are terrified of losing control, but a few tears and days off work now are better than something more serious at a later date. Remember, feelings cannot be wiped away. They are a real force, and if you are a true realist and genuinely capable of ordering your life you will recognise this fact. It is common sense to admit when you need help and to seek it. No, friends cannot mend a broken romance, but do not underestimate the importance of talking, crying, mourning – and healing. You can get over this, but not by pretending it isn't there.

Starting afresh

This is something that many Virgos struggle with. Once your sense of trust is breached it may be hard to love again. Besides, the reluctance of Virgos to mourn may block the way to any genuine moving forwards. You may prefer to wed yourself to your work. You need to give yourself plenty of time to get over a hurt and also to be very honest with yourselves when you form a new relationship, for you may assess the new lover on the basis of the old and sow the seeds of discord by expecting trouble when it isn't even in the air. Failure and loneliness can send the Virgoan critical propensity into overdrive. Occasionally, bereft Virgos fancy that they are physically ill and use new partners as a nurse, resenting any emotional demands that they may make. This is unfair – and unrealistic.

Virgos need to give themselves plenty of time to get over a failed romance and to recover their autonomy. Remember what it was like before he or she came along? You were fine then, were you not? You can find that sense of happiness and independence again, and it is most important that you do so if you are to make successful relationships in the future. But try to ensure that this is genuine independence, not something built on bitterness. You owe this to yourself and future partners.

■ PRACTICE AND CHANGE ■

- You may need to remind yourself that your passion for accuracy may get in the way of your passionate relationships – and they are more important, in truth. Try not to make remarks that those you love may experience as critical.
- It is more important for you to learn to cope with emotions – both your own and others'. If emotional displays frighten you then you need to ask yourself why. If you are afraid of what may be unleashed in yourself then you have better prospects of being in true control if you know what you are dealing with. As for the feelings of others – why should these make you uneasy? You can help, and make a person you care for feel better if you will learn how.
- Although you are a serious and subdued person for the most part there is no doubt that you need romance, play and even a little excitement. Do not shut these out of your life when they arrive.
- The sexual side of relationships is very important to you. Do not let your search for control and knowledge suffocate your sensual side.
- In general, remind yourself to loosen up a little. The world will not come to wrack and ruin, and neither will your life, if you allow yourself to be spontaneous on occasion.
- Never allow your sense of guilt and responsibility to make a doormat of you. Guilt is never a helpful emotion, because it is self-destructive. Take responsibility in due measure and set yourself free of the rest.
- Always remind yourself, that although you hate to be helped, it is what you, and everyone else needs at times. Have the courage to let others help you, when occasion demands.

3 ♍ All in the family

Accidents will occur in the best-regulated families

Charles Dickens, Mr Micawber in *David Copperfield*

A Virgo in the family is often a stabilising influence, bringing balance and common sense to fraught situations. Virgos do not like scenes and they can rarely put up with chaos. The calm presence of Virgo can be very soothing. However, Virgos themselves will get most upset and worried by lack of stability. Let's take a look at Virgo in some of the traditional family roles.

■ VIRGO MOTHER

In motherhood as all else, control is important to this lady. For this reason she is less likely to have an unplanned baby than most, and will usually ensure that she has only the number of children that she can cope with easily and efficiently. Many Virgos limit their families to one or two children. Ms Virgo often feels little need for children as an expression of her womanhood – she fulfils this in other, less obtrusive but just as concrete ways. However, children having arrived on the scene, Virgo mother will give them the most meticulous care of which she is capable in every area of their lives.

It is rare to see the offspring of Virgo mother in torn jeans and trainers coming apart at the soles – unless, that is, she's one of the very 'Earthy' types, who has decided such trifles don't matter. She will have noticed them, make no mistake. It's just that she prefers to accept the fact that 'children will be children' and devote her time to making nettle soup or preparing a thesaurus. It is more likely that the children of Virgo mother will have faces shiny from recently wielded soap and flannel, shoes neatly laced and polished and cardigans done up to the neck. I have known Virgo mums who were fussy to the point of neurosis about their children's cleanliness, rushing to the sink with every speck of mud, but I have also known the more relaxed variety. Probably this depends on what other matters occupy Virgo mother's time, for if she is fulfilled by an interesting job, or other occupation, she is less likely to go overboard into the bathtub, so to speak. Virgo mum will prefer to have paid work, for she likes to feel that finances are to some extent under her control. However, she is most unlikely to overstretch her time, unless there are considerable financial pressures. She likes to plan, so that she can do everything properly, and will drive herself to the brink trying to be Superwoman, rather than leave beds unmade and homework unsupervised.

This mum is gentle and her love is profound. The only drawback is that she may forget to show it, her priorities being hygiene, nutrition and organisation. She is often an excellent cook, and devoted to the safety and well-being of her children, and in this she may need to be careful, for she may find it hard to let her children make mistakes and skin their knees. She needs to remind herself that experience is the best teacher, and beyond sensible boundaries to let her children find out about life in its rough and tumble. She cannot always expect them to take her excellent advice. In addition, she does need to remind herself not to be too critical, for what she may intend as a word of kindly advice may be interpreted as a heavy putdown by Junior.

Virgo mum isn't slow to tell other mums that their offspring are transgressing. Nor will she fail to point out the superior talents of her own infant prodigy. Virgo, so slow to boast for itself, is much quicker off the mark where the children are concerned. This arises from a touching pride, and may be Virgo's way of expressing love, but it can alienate other parents. Virgo mother needs to give herself a nudge when it come to giving hugs and having fun with her kids. They shouldn't just be read a goodnight story because it will help them value books – read to them merely for the joy of it, stories that you and they will love. This mum is one of the most exemplary in the zodiac, and all she needs to do to attain near-perfection is to loosen up just a little. Her children should keep their room tidy, show her that they listen to her, buy her fragrant flowers in pots, and try to get her to have a giggle occasionally. Oh, and when all the housework and homework is done, snuggle up to her and have a cuddle. She needs it as much as they do!

■ VIRGO FATHER

It would be interesting at some point to examine the statistics for vasectomies, related to Sun sign, for most Virgo men I have encountered have had one sooner rather than later! Virgo is rarely an enthusiastic dad, probably because as real to him as the cuddly pink bundle in his arms are the many sleepless nights, dirty nappies and large bills for laundry, food, education, clothes . . . You can see the balance sheet printing out behind the rather worried Virgoan eyes. Not that this father isn't loving – he is. He takes an Earth-sign satisfaction in the renewal of the species in his image, although he is never so interested in 'carrying on the family name' as Capricorn may be. Like Virgo mother his love is deep and caring. And like her he doesn't show it.

Virgo dad can easily be made to feel guilty if his children seem to have less of life's advantages than others, and so he will do his hard-working best to provide clothes and food of excellent quality, funds for holidays (especially educational ones, or those organised by the school) and money for extra-curricular activities. He helps painstakingly with homework, and teaches his child all the skills of which he is master, and although he is actually very patient he may came across as irrascible simply because he is trying so hard and sacrificing his free time. He may also be critical and impatient with youngsters, especially dreamy ones, or those who are 'all fingers and thumbs'. Like Virgo mum he needs to relax and learn to enjoy his children.

Discipline may be important to this dad – he likes good behaviour. The Virgoan prudishness may peep out in regard to offspring, and this can be most in evidence in a father, who was no better than any Earth sign should be in his youth, being extra watchful when it comes to the sexuality of his growing daughter. Virgos in these situations need to use their common sense and worldly wisdom to foster acceptance in themselves and to give gentle advice and support – not to proscribe, criticise or make guilty young people who have to experience life for themselves. The hard bit here is that Virgo knows so well all the things that can go wrong that it may be agony to stand and watch. Grit your teeth – it doesn't last forever!

Every Virgo dad should concentrate from the start on forming a close bond with his children. His insistence on practicalities, moderation, safety and all the other Virgoan priorities may mean that the most important element of all – affection – goes a-begging. Really, the most valuable thing that Virgo dad (and mum, for that matter) can do for their kids is learn *from* them. They are the finest opportunity you will ever have to experience spontaneity, laughter and fun, first hand.

■ THE VIRGO CHILD

At the start of this chapter we mentioned the need in Virgo for a stable environment, and this is especially true of the Virgo child.

♍ All in the family ♍

Noise, upheaval, insecurity, emotional storms and an unpredictable family scene will do this child more harm than most. Little Virgo is one of those who needs a routine. He or she also needs lots of cuddles – not forced embraces, but gentle, open arms always offered. This child also needs appreciation as much as food. Virgo will rarely court the spotlight but there is a yearning within to be noticed and valued. These types often feel they have less to offer than their more ebullient cousins, and if this isn't remedied by obvious and continuous commendation in youth they may grow up with an inferiority complex of sorts.

Never violate the bodyspace of these children by insisting they eat what they do not want, wear what feels uncomfortable (Virgos are often very sensitive to texture and colour) or kiss Aunt Maud goodnight if they do not want to. Virgos will not wish to protest openly (although getting food into their closed mouths will be more difficult than fixing a screw into a wall, and very cruel to both of you). Indeed, all children need to be given the space to declare their own bodily needs from as early as possible – for instance, we all have vastly different metabolic rates, so how can even the wisest mum know just how much food her child requires? Little Virgo will know exactly what he or she needs, and this should be respected. Virgos are especially sensitive to control, and interference of this intimate sort and coercion may court eating disorders in later life, as Virgo overcompensates and reclaims control. Always remember that privacy, integrity and dignity are especially important to Virgo.

This child should not be criticised, except in as mild as possible a manner, and never loudly or in public, for this would be crushing. If you need to rebuke young Virgo then ensure that it is the action that is called in question, not the child. (For example, to say 'That wasn't a good idea, was it? Maybe you need to think more about such actions in the future,' is a far cry from saying 'You're stupid.

♍ VIRGO ♍

Make sure you learn.') Where possible encourage little Virgos to comment upon their own work and get them to see the good bits. However, Virgo can be somewhat precocious and may, in the nicest, most well-spoken way, sometimes correct adults! If you want your child to be liked, this isn't something to be encouraged! Point out that this is a disrespectful and impolite way to act, and that Virgo would not like it if the boot were on the other foot!

Virgo children must have the best education you can afford – follow up all their talents as best you can, and don't think that because this is rarely a dreamy child that he or she isn't creative, for many Virgos make excellent musicians, artists and poets. Let Virgos give a hand around the house as early as possible – they will like to have their own jobs to do. Help Virgos to make the most of their practicality and quiet affectionate nature by giving them small pets – rabbits or guinea pigs are often favoured. When adolescence arrives above all do not embarrass your Virgo by awkward questions or – heaven forbid – jokes! Give them the opportunity to groom themselves without any comment from you. Always give them the opportunity to talk by showing that you are prepared *really* to listen, and do avoid lectures, otherwise much will go on that you never hear about. Sensitive handling at this point will ensure that your Virgo sons or daughters, with all their native discrimination and common sense, grow up able to handle life better than most. Make them feel awkward and they just may, to prove a point, go enough against their nature to do something regrettable.

In your Virgo sons or daughters you are most fortunate, for here are sensible, practical youngsters who need all your love to bring out their best. Give it unstintingly and they will reward you by being useful members of society and the family, and giving you all the quiet, enduring warmth of their affection.

♍ All in the family ♍

■ VIRGO AS SIBLINGS

If you are one of the more ramshackle signs of the zodiac – that is, all the other eleven – you may find an older brother or sister with sun in Virgo a tough act to follow. Your older Virgo sibling may make you feel small by knowing all the answers, and it may be impossible to believe that this paragon is not the most confident person on Earth. He or she isn't. Show your older Virgo how much you admire what he or she does (even if it chokes you!) and you may be rewarded by a warmth you'd not expected, and lots of help where you need it. If Virgo follows you in the family, take care of this little one. Yes, you might be driven mad when he or she tells Mum that you've brought mud in *again*, but Virgos only try so hard to do what's right because they are always so terrified of being wrong. Losing your temper with them will only make them worse – for Virgo can be contrary. Let them enter your older world as much as possible, for they are dying to learn. With any luck they will be willing to help you with chores, if you show enough appreciation. If the relationship between you is good, your Virgo sibling can grow to be your best, and most helpful friend.

■ VIRGO IN THE HOME

This is not generally a sign that needs to 'spread itself' over the whole house and the living space of others. Virgos generally like to keep their things neat, where they can find them, and where they will be safe. It is most important for this sign to have privacy as early as possible and to feel that there is a place for their own belongings where no one else will intrude. This is part of the 'inviolability' of Virgo. Do your best to let Virgo have his is her own room, or cleverly use partitions, if this is not possible. Virgo should have lots of cleverly planned cupboards where there will be nooks and crannies for

VIRGO

treasures – a drawer for pens and crayons, another for modelling clay – keeping it all neat and sorted. Of course, Virgo will also need space for whatever musical instrument or other kit is required for his or her interests. Virgo is actually a sign that, unobtrusively, can take up quite a lot of space, because Virgos are so keen to involve themselves with life. The best that others in the family can do is to ensure that order and tidiness are possible in the set-up – Virgo won't want just one large cupboard in which to throw everything. Most Virgos also prefer to avoid violent colour schemes. Quieter hues are more soothing to them, and will make the place look larger.

♍ All in the family ♍

■ PRACTICE AND CHANGE ■

- Do not let accusations of 'selfish' induce you to have more children than your comfort will countenance.
- Affection is the most important thing that you can give your child. It's not that this isn't a loving sign – it's just that showing it may be low on the scale of priorities. Add 'cuddles' to your daily list.
- Children can teach you how to play. Be prepared to learn from your children, as well as to teach them.
- Virgo children should be given the minimum of criticism, but they should also, kindly but firmly, be discouraged from criticising others.
- Try to relax and do not to expect too much, either from yourself or your little ones.
- Although Virgo children are not usually dreamy, encourage them to be creative. Read this child fairy stories and explain that imagination is a creative faculty, standing behind everything made by humans from symphonies to motorways. Show them that imagination is *useful* – then they may cultivate it.
- Virgos can never be 'spoilt' by too much attention and praise, but always praise sensibly, or Virgo will not take you seriously.
- The best thing you can do with living space, for Virgo, is to give the opportunity for tidiness, order, cleanliness and simplicity. Avoid clutter and overbearing colour schemes, and let young Virgos make suggestions and even help with the decorating. They are likely to be very practical and may have some useful ideas.

4 Friendships and the single life

A faithful friend is the medicine of life

Ecclesiasticus, 6:16

Friendships are naturally important to all of us, whether we are married or single. However, those who are single may find they have more time to devote to friends. Because Virgo is earnest about most undertakings, some Virgos may find it hard to keep up what they see as the standards required in a partnership – time spent together, sharing and caring – and to give attention also to their friends. Sometimes Virgos may shrink their social activities when in a partnership. This is a shame, as you need to interact with a variety of people because your minds are active and versatile.

■ VIRGO AS A FRIEND

Those chosen by you as a friend should take it as a great compliment. Virgos regard their time as valuable and you won't waste it on someone whose mind is turgid and whose conversation is narrow. This sign likes mental stimulation, and you like common sense. You are great mates if friends want help in planning an event, such as a picnic, and you just love it if they ask your advice. You are sure to be a mine of information about something – friends should find out what it is and pick your brains. Many Virgos are very interested in health, hygiene and nutrition and will enjoy talking about that – your knowledge may be extensive. Virgos do tend to choose most of

Friendships and the single life

their friends from work colleagues, because then it is certain that one important thing is held in common. Indeed, many Virgos rarely meet new friends outside work, possibly because there is not the time. Friendship, to Virgo, is a serious pursuit.

Virgo will give friends tea in abundance – probably Earl Grey or a herbal variety – and sympathy in moderation. You love to help, but yours is a practical approach and you may not be talented with empathy. In fact, you may not be sure what it is, exactly, for as far as you are concerned, if there's a problem then there must be a way to fix it. Simply 'being' with someone who is upset may seem useless to you, and you feel secretly threatened by it unless you have learnt that your emotional support and your simple presence is useful in a more subtle fashion. You are very positive in your approach. However, you will like friends to take your advice, and you may remark pointedly upon the fact they haven't, especially if you are shown to be right – Virgo is not above 'I told you so'. Your sign likes to help those who help themselves.

Too much sweet talk can make Virgo quite queasy, for it smacks of insincerity, which is anathema. This sign would far rather hurt friends with honesty than take them in by lying, and if you are too complimentary it just doesn't sound right to you – after all, we know nothing can be that good. When my Virgo friend commented on my new hairdo by saying 'Your hair looks much better like that,' it sounded anything but flattering. Better! Better than what? Presumably my usual trailing locks were 'bad' and this was simply 'better'. It didn't exactly give me a warm glow, but it wasn't meant that way. Nor was it intended to hurt. Virgo just meant exactly what she said – I looked 'better'.

Once the friendship is established some Virgos have been known to assume *carte blanche* to sort out their friends' lives. You may rearrange their paperwork, clear their kitchen and book them in for that Semantics lecture, that looks so interesting (to you!). This is the way that some Virgos express their concern and their caring. After all, it is practical. Virgo, having given the matter deep and clear thought, does not question the assessment. Now some people, of course, will find this very trying, but it is truly meant in a kindly way. It may be a rather uptight way of saying 'I care about you'. Friends should try not to misunderstand it, or treat it roughly, for despite the fact it looks very 'managing', as a Virgo you probably lack confidence and spontaneity, and this is the only way you know to express warmth. Friends should treat this with kindness and firmness if it occurs. Of course, most Virgos aren't nearly so invasive. Yours is a diffident reserved sign and while your Earthiness may encourage you to physical contact – pats on the hand or a gentle embrace of welcome – you are never sure of approval. Whatever the case, friends should treat you gently. A Virgo friend has so much to offer, and you are never sure of your value. Remember, your dislike of compliments doesn't apply when you are on the receiving end, and while you may disclaim and discount, deep within you something is blossoming.

■ VIRGO AND THE SINGLE LIFE

Virgo needs seclusion and sometimes you take very well to the single state. It gives you time to ponder on what is of importance, and it leaves more space for the all-important work. Virgos often have a vague feeling of rejection, and because of this it may seem easier to keep away from other people. However, if this is taken too far it becomes a self-fulfiling belief. You need to be aware that you may be repeating patterns that invite rejection – helping too much, advising where not consulted or merely being over-reserved – and that if these can be changed you can find approval. Virgo often tries too hard, concentrating on the practical and forgetting the feelings of others. However, while you do need plenty of space to sort, meditate and reflect, you do not relish being solitary. It is far more important to you to be useful members of society. You need and deserve a place.

♍ Friendships and the single life ♍

This sign is often committed to personal growth of one sort or another. If you are a single Virgo then do ensure that you are involved in community activities, workshops, lectures – anything that interests you. Maintain a sense of proportion about your work, for it should not be the whole of your life. Be prepared also to make compromises. I know you would rather be alone than spend time with those with whom you have nothing in common, but give people a chance. There is a niche for you, and your approach – give yourself a chance also.

■ PRACTICE AND CHANGE ■

- Try to ensure that your social orbit extends beyond your partner, if you have one. You need variety.
- Ensure that work does not overwhelm your social life or form your only source of friendship.
- Offer your advice tactfully and try to ignore it, if it isn't taken. This isn't a personal affront or a rejection of your common sense – it is human nature.
- If you can pay a sincere compliment, do so from time to time. It will become easier with practice, and it melts people's hearts.
- Remember that you cannot sort out the lives of others – they have to make their own mistakes.
- Make time in your life for the necessary degree of seclusion. You need this time to reflect and sort things out.
- If you want to expand your social circle, offer your services in some respect. Make people welcome with your knowledge of creature comforts. Never tell yourself you have little to offer or that you aren't interesting. You are one of the most interesting, subtle signs of the zodiac, so give people a chance to find this out.

5  Career

The purpose of life is not to be happy – but to be productive, to be useful

Leo Rosten

Virgo is the sign of the workaholic. Next to the typical Virgo even Capricorn may look like a lounge lizard. Work in some form is the very stuff of Virgo's life and you have an intense need to feel you are useful, productive and of service. In truth many a Virgo lives to work, rather than works to live. Even Virgos who really are not desperate for money still feel the drive to be gainfully employed. This may in part be due to anxiety about what is around the corner. It may also be connected to the Virgo belief that 'the devil makes work for idle hands' – what this really means is that the devil, in terms of myriad anxieties, is likely to beset the minds of Virgos who are unoccupied!

Virgo is not an ambitious sign, nor do you usually covet wealth for its own sake – although this isn't always the case. What Virgo prizes above all is self-sufficiency. Virgo likes to feel safe in the knowledge that rainy days are well provided for by a solid roof of job security, savings and investment. This is not a sign that trusts in life or the welfare state to provide in sickness and old age. Industrious, independent and provident, Virgo likes to be busy, in work and out of debt. Female Virgos do sometimes make a 'job' out of running a house and family, and may feel fulfilled by this. Mostly, however, Virgo feels much better when actively earning.

TRADITIONAL VIRGO CAREERS

The common denominator for all occupations suitable for Virgos is that they require practicality, a painstaking and analytical approach, and many of them are specifically to do with public services. Virgo careers include:

- editor
- secretary
- clerical work
- scientist
- lab technician
- statistician
- proofreader
- teacher
- accountant
- caterer
- gardener
- craftsperson
- inspector
- hygiene and/or nutrition specialist
- psychologist
- technologist
- nurse
- critic

WHAT TO LOOK FOR IN YOUR WORK

The great majority of people work in large insurance corporations, sales offices, shops, banks and factories. Relatively few of us can choose a profession, train for it and find a fulfilling lifestyle, and as time progresses this is becoming more elusive.

To help you find a job that suits you, you need to bear in mind the spirit of what is recommended, not the specific occupation. One office job is not like another, one job selling fashions may differ enormously from one down the street in terms of environment and opportunity. As a Virgo you need to make sure of several things when seeking employment:
- Ensure that what you will be doing, your schedule, environment and colleagues will be mostly predictable. Virgos are resourceful,

VIRGO

and some of you do respond particularly to the mutable character of the sign in adapting to change, but most are far more comfortable if there are few surprises.

- You will not be called upon to be high profile. Few Virgos enjoy the spotlight, or any exposed or up-front position.
- Industry and attention to detail will be valued by your employer and rewarded.
- You will be needed and appreciated, and *told* so.
- The job is well and reliably paid. Never rely on bonuses.
- There will be enough for you to do. You will not be happy standing around filing your nails and reading magazines, even if you are being paid handsomely for doing so.
- There are enough demands on your resourcefulness. Predictability is one thing, no challenge *at all* is another, and you will be wasted if you don't have to come up with interesting and practical solutions.

From this you can see that there is no need to feel that you have to look for a specifically Virgoan job. Many Virgos wouldn't have a clue what to do in a lab and wouldn't much relish the thought of getting all grubby in a market garden. Look for something that suits in its content and atmosphere, rather than its label. If it isn't right, plan carefully and make changes.

■ FINGER-IN-THE-DYKE

Most people have heard the story of the little Dutch boy who kept back the waters that were threatening to engulf his village by standing with his finger blocking the leak in the dyke. Such devotion to duty, such patience and responsibility (not to mention courage) are very much Virgoan themes. Many Virgos go through life with the vague but perpetual feeling that they do have their finger stuck in some metaphorical dyke, and that if they withdraw it all hell will break loose. This is often seen graphically in the people who act as if the entire hospital/corporation/hotel/bank will come to wrack and ruin if they ease up for one moment on their efforts. Always in motion, always frowning, usually preoccupied (but never absent minded concerning the job in hand) working late until ten or eleven, and at weekends, too, for the most part, this 'workaholic' has a very serious addiction indeed. Finger-in-the-dyke may believe that he or she is indispensable, and there is very little doubt that he or she is extremely useful. However, if this person were to stop work tomorrow the truth of the matter is that everything would jog along much as usual, in the way that it would if any lesser mortals were to fall by the wayside. Finger-in-the-dyke is actually desperately fending off tides of self-doubt, self-destructive criticism and a general feeling of worthlessness. These people may well make everyone else feel very guilty, lazy and worthless, and that is how *they* feel inside. If Finger-in-the-dyke is part of an organisation, others should be patient. He or she may make colleagues feel small and give them some very short answers, but an unhappy soul lurks behind that wrinkled brow.

If you are a Finger-in-the-dyke, at some point you will need to face up to whatever it is inside you that you are avoiding. The sad truth is that you, like anyone else, may one day be made redundant – because, you see, no one *is* that indispensable, however hard they work. All work and no play makes Jack not only a dull boy but also potentially a sick boy. Learn to find some value in yourself, for yourself, not by working your butt off for something that would go on without you – that is above and beyond the call of duty. Turn your scrupulous attention to your own health and well-being and reassess your life with a keen and dispassionate eye. It has much more to offer you than endless striving.

VIRGO

■ THE CRITIC

This is a common face of Virgo, and we cannot get through a chapter without addressing it in connection with each theme!

The Critic in the workplace is she or he who seems to find a *raison d'être* in pulling apart everything that everyone else ever does. A true Critic leaves no spelling mistakes unremarked, comments on the state of each person's desk and watches the clock at the end of every lunch hour, carefully counting the extra seconds taken by everyone.

The Critic may be your boss, in which case you're in trouble. Best move on. However, the Critic is more likely a colleague who has a chip on his or her shoulders. There are two choices. Either ignore this person, in the sure knowledge that there is something lacking, that others are far more creative and will soon be streets ahead of the Critic – or retaliate.

Those who choose the latter option had better be good. How well-organised, punctual and accurate can they be? And how observant are they? The Critic is sure to make mistakes – everyone does – and if colleagues are up for it they can make it their business to find out all the mistakes and comment on them in minute detail. Is it really worth it wasting time that way, because the risk is of becoming becalmed in a noxious little backwater, like the Critic. Perhaps this person is best ignored.

If you are the Critic, why, oh why are you wasting all that fine discrimination and that talent for analysis simply getting everyone's back up? Does it really make you feel good? I am sure it cannot. So get out of the acid bath and get a life. Your talent for observation can be put to much better use. 'Positive' must be your keyword from now on, and if you apply it you won't recognise your situation in a few years' time.

THE VIRGO BOSS

Needless to say, this boss is unlikely to tolerate lack of punctuality or anything slapdash. In truth the Virgo boss is often rather uptight – it rarely suits Virgo to be captain of the ship, you prefer the post of First Mate, where you can concentrate on details rather then the grand plan. A Virgo who is constantly trying to discern the wood when all that can be seen are the trees is a Virgo with a perpetual headache. However, many Virgos by virtue of their industry and capability do find themselves in positions of responsibility, and employees may well find themselves answerable to a rather edgy Virgo.

If employees have more vision than their Virgo boss, they should share their ideas humbly, never trying to make Virgo feel small or – dare I say it – criticising – for they will get very short shrift. Virgo will size them up and will certainly try to use their talents to best advantage. Virgo may certainly entertain their bright ideas but will pare them down so mercilessly they may hardly recognise them – but the ideas will be *workable*. Virgo will be grateful, and won't forget these efforts.

Employees should not expect large rises, swift promotion or huge presents and bonuses. Virgo will pay them what they're worth, and if they prove themselves that should rise steadily. Virgo boss won't believe any cock-and-bull stories, for he or she is so practical and very realistic about human nature the stories will be seen through with clarity that seems almost clairvoyant, though it is anything but. Virgo may understand genuine sick leave, but employees shouldn't try to leave early to purchase an outfit for the wedding they're going to on Saturday – such fripperies will get them a very bad name. And they mustn't for goodness sake, flirt or gossip behind the filing cabinet! If there is anything that can shorten the Virgo fuse, it's silly whispering and giggling when there's a job to do and Virgo's *worrying* about it!

♍ VIRGO ♍

Employees should work hard for their Virgo boss, keep their nails clean, their desk tidy, and stay ten minutes longer when they can. Show this boss they are reliable, sensible and useful and they will find just how kind this person can be. Uncannily observant, Virgo will notice if they are out of sorts and may well send them home.

Virgo boss will reward their efforts in due measure and give them the benefit of their help and advice from time to time. With Virgo's life experience that's worth a great deal!

■ THE VIRGO EMPLOYEE

This person may speedily bid fair to be the jewel in the work force, but an employer shouldn't be too quick to tell him or her. It's not that Virgos don't need praise, for we all know they do. It's just that if an employer is in too much of a hurry, Virgo will smell a rat, even if there isn't a rodent for miles. Virgo employees should be promoted slowly – they need time to adjust – and, yes, you've guessed, don't criticise.

It is likely that Virgo will be a most reliable, painstaking, thorough and efficient employee. Virgos are rarely an asset in sales, unless the emphasis is on service. Trying to sell ice to Eskimos deeply offends their sense of truth and usefulness and they may seize up under the effort. These people are intelligent, painstaking and versatile – yes, they just love to be useful. Secretly they need to be told they are valued and special, and without this they will wilt and fade, slowly. Not so secretly, they desire fair and reliable pay, and without this they will quit, quickly. Never think because they are painstaking that they are slow, for their brains are swift and sharp as lasers, and they can size everything up and act like lightning if they have to – but they would rather not.

Virgo employees will gain speed and momentum as they acquire confidence. They should be allowed to carve out a niche for themselves. They miss nothing – especially not a long, liquid lunch that their sensitive nose will detect as colleagues wander in, very mellow, at 3:30 p.m. In due time, Virgo should be elevated to a position of responsibility – not at the top of the tree but as one of its principal branches. Virgo employees won't be dazzling, but just watch them glow!

WHEN UNEMPLOYMENT STRIKES

This is bad news indeed for Virgos, who can worry themselves into an early grave if they are out of work. However, this happens so frequently these days that not even Virgoan industry can ensure job safety, so if you are a Virgo facing unemployment try to be realistic. This is one of the facts of life, and you need to face it. Don't panic.

In the first place you may need to resign yourself to some time spent out of work, so do not expect to get a job straight away or you will only become more upset if you fail. This does not mean there is anything wrong with you, it just means you need to go on trying – and you never were a quitter.

Focus all your organisational and your analytical skills on getting a job. Turn finding a job into a job itself. Make lists, schedules and plans, and work hard through each day as if you really were in paid employment. Make lists also of your talents, for there may be resources that you can draw upon that you have forgotten about – you know how you underestimate yourself, or you should know by now if you have read and digested earlier pages.

One thing is certain, there is *no doubt* that you will get another job – tell this to yourself when you lie awake at night. This has nothing to do with misplaced faith in an unreliable universe or falsely positive thinking or 'living in cloud-cuckoo land'. It is a simple fact that you will get another job, because you have always worked hard and shown your efficiency. You are doing so now, as you look for work, and you will do so again when you find it.

■ SELF-EMPLOYMENT AND OTHER MATTERS

Not all work relies on a company and an employer, for there are many other approaches. In general, however, it suits Virgo better to enter a concern that is already established. Unless there is a lot of Fire in your chart, it may be hard for you to envision a scheme and a future for your enterprise, and you may find that you get bogged down by details. Also it is all too easy for you to think up reasons *not* to do things, rather than reasons to do them. So if you are thinking about becoming self-employed, it is probably a good idea to consult someone who has some sort of proven record in getting such concerns off the ground. So much the better if you can go into partnership with another person who will supply some of the initiative and ideas. If you do go it alone, taking out a franchise or starting in a small way is far better than anything more large scale and risky, which you will probably avoid anyway.

■ PRACTICE AND CHANGE ■

- Remember that workaholism can be just as dangerous as other addictions. Generally, you are careful about your health, so avoid excess in this as in other matters. If you are losing yourself in work, ask yourself, in your penetrating, analytical way, what you are afraid of finding – or what do you fear will find *you* – if you have leisure. Do not be content with a quick or facile answer.

- As your work is so important to you, put plenty of effort into ensuring that your job is satisfying, not just 'okay' – you deserve better. Your work should enable you to be and feel useful and productive. You need as much security as is realistic, and your earnings should be good and reliable. Ensure you will be appreciated by those for whom you work, and that your resourcefulness will be needed and used. Also make sure that there will be plenty for you to do – you hate to be bored, and daydreaming is not your favourite activity!

- If you find yourself on a power trip of criticising others, realise that this is a dead end. What imagined inadequacy are you compensating for? Use your analytical talents to work for your future, not to soothe some chip on your shoulder, which can be only temporary. Make 'Be positive' your motto.

- No one is indispensable, not even you – and no one ever said, on their death bed, that they wish they'd spent more time at the office. Decide what is really of value to you and give yourself the time and the permission to enjoy it.

6 Healthy, wealthy – and wise?

If you're a hypochondriac, first class, you awaken each morning with the firm resolve not to worry; everything is going to turn out all wrong

Goodman Ace

■ HEALTH

Astrological reflections on health, even when based on the entire chart, are not always helpful, for health is dependent on so many different factors. What may we usefully say about the health of Virgo in general?

Of all the zodiacal signs, Virgo is the one most concerned with health. Many Virgos are well informed generally about health matters, and some are quite expert in related areas, for instance regarding natural therapies, herbs and first aid. It is important for you to be prepared and efficient, and looking after the body often seems to you the most practical and sensible of studies.

You like to improve yourself by diet and exercise, and many Virgos will plan and employ considerable thought and self-discipline. Virgoan discrimination and aesthetic sense are here beautifully manifested, but like anything else, this can get out of balance.

Some Virgos are prone to hypochondria. Being very aware of the body you may attach excessive importance to small symptoms, and a mere sniffle can set you scouring through 'The Encyclopaedia of Family Health' and associated volumes. Occasionally, Virgos are so fascinated by their bodily processes that they feel impelled to

♍ Healthy, wealthy – and wise? ♍

recount them always and in detail. A friend of mine, married to a Virgo, swears he has not once in their entire married life been to the toilet without describing to her exactly the workings of his bowels. This sign is capable of graphic detail!

One of the main problems associated with Virgo is worry, and that can produce all sorts of symptoms. The symptoms then produce more worry, and so on, until you can, in extreme cases, become really ill. If you are a Virgo caught in this cycle, you should go to the doctor immediately you become worried, rather than let it fester. If this means you are going nearly every week, then you need more occupation for an active mind and should find it without delay.

Virgos are often particular about food. Some will examine each lettuce leaf under a microscope, looking for specks of dirt (but the 'Earthy' variety will buy organic and wash it minimally). Others demand epicure standard in each mouthful or select carefully only that which doesn't upset their stomachs.

While prone to a spare figure, Virgos do occasionally overeat, and weight problems from 'comfort eating' are a possibility. This sign, prone to self-denial, fretting and overwork may well seek solace in the reliable food cupboard. Naturally, if this happens, the source of stress needs to be tracked down, for overweight will only cause more worry.

The typical Virgoan appearance (perhaps more in evidence as a Rising Sign) is not robust, although wiry. Virgos may appear to be relatively weak children but their strength tends to increase with age. Virgos are rarely full-blown 'health freaks', for this tendency belongs more to Fire signs and those less well-connected with physical reality. However, worry and nervous exhaustion are especially likely to afflict Virgos and, with your realistic natures, you should do your best to protect yourselves from this.

Allergies and upset stomachs

No one can be quite sure of the origins of allergies, but Virgo, with its tendency to sensitivity, is often prone to them. Virgo is said to rule the abdominal region, spleen, intestines and nerves. Coupled with the tendency to worry, this may give rise to such complaints as ulcers and general nervous disorders. Lousie Hay in *You Can Heal Your Life* points out that problems with the spleen relate to obsessions – a Virgoan preoccupation!

The best approach to these matters derives from Virgo's own talents – learn about health in a positive way and apply knowledge in balance. This sign, especially, needs to moderate the tendency to overwork. This can be difficult, because some Virgos worry so much when they aren't working that this is counter-productive. Hypnotherapy and relaxation therapy can help. If you can learn to meditate you will greatly benefit from the detachment and peace.

MONEY

This is one of the signs that is 'good' with money. Some Virgos claim proudly that they have never owed a penny in their lives, and will emit pious phrases, such as 'Neither a borrower nor a lender be' which is actually very good advice. Some Virgos are good at juggling finances and robbing Peter to pay Paul, but they are seldom contented doing this. It preys on their minds and they have nightmares about the entire card-castle falling down around their ears, which is unlikely due to their precision.

Virgo likes to be in control of things, and finances are no exception. However, although this is an Earth sign, it is also a Mutable one. Because of this Virgo is often a little less at ease than Capricorn and Taurus, who, while they may be provident, make little less of a 'meal' of it. Because of the changeability of Virgo – displayed in the quick reactions and sensitivity – you are also aware of the changeability of the cosmos, and in particular the unreliability of the pound or dollar.

Virgos are afraid of being dependent or penniless when you are ill or getting older, and because of this you are particular about insurance policies and investments. Of course, Virgos also like to be generous to friends and family, and you are aware that this will not be possible if you do not work everything out and budget.

Unless there is a substantial proportion of Fire in the chart, the only 'problem' likely with money is that old beastie, worry. There does come a point where Virgo must relinquish control and be prepared to trust that the universe will provide what is necessary. Virgos also need to trust in their own resourcefulness, for if the unforeseen does arise there is no sign more likely to be able to cope than Virgo.

WISDOM

Virgo wisdom is of the practical type. You know the value of a task in life and of tangible results. At your best you demonstrate the good sense of taking life in bite-size pieces and chewing each mouthful properly. A balanced Virgo has all the exquisite serenity of a Chinese painting. Virgo says 'Don't try the impossible. Concentrate on the workable and the useful, and do it well.' Virgo knows also, in the words of Keats that 'truth is beauty, beauty is truth'. The simplicity and precision of this sign has an aesthetic quality.

♍ VIRGO ♍

■ PRACTICE AND CHANGE ■

Health

- Make sure you are well informed about the positive aspects of healthcare, such as nutrition and lifestyle, and apply this knowledge. Unless you are a professional, avoid becoming a mine of information about symptoms and their possible meanings, for this is an invitation to excessive worry.
- Plan to include some relaxing and thoroughly enjoyable activities in your life. This will mean that your only comfort does not reside in food.
- Learn to relax. This is a physical technique and a matter of awareness and control, so it is well within your grasp. Hypnotherapy is also invaluable for learning to relax.
- Allergy testing is available in many natural therapy clinics. You may wish to take advantage of this.

Money

- The fear that makes you hang on to your cash may be standing between you and good fortune – a kind of subtle signalling system that says 'Nothing gets past here' – and that will include the good things. If that seems too irrational, consider body language. We pick up a myriad of unspoken facts about others, unconsciously, just by being with them for moments. If you are uptight and closed fisted, people will sense your lack of trust, they may not trust you in turn and you may miss opportunities. Open out, and be prepared to give – then you will also receive.

7 ♍ Style and leisure

The busiest men have the most leisure

Nineteenth-century proverb

■ YOUR LEISURE

If the quotation above were always true then Virgo would be the most leisurely of signs. However, Virgo is all too apt to fill all leisure time with jobs – and sometimes this means the actual paid job. This sign gets anxious if there isn't anything to do and you may cast about you for repair jobs or sorting and tidying, rather than sit idle. Although it is true that Virgo does enjoy work and gets a deep glow of satisfaction from doing it well, there has to be a limit.

For Virgo, relaxation should involve some industry – this sign is not good at doing nothing. Some people may feel that this isn't healthy, but each to his own. As long as the occupation doesn't mean you sit with furrowed brow and hunched shoulders; as long as it does not entail grind and pressure, then it is fine, and to be recommended. You are often good at crafts, and may produce some lovely things in your 'spare' time. Hobbies can include gardening, cooking and DIY. Most people benefit from a walk, but this is especially true of Virgo, who has an unspoken kinship with the earth and all that grows. You sense the life and sentience all around, not in a sentimental way, but strongly and realistically. Contact with nature is very soothing to you, and many Virgos love to keep pets or look after animals. If you have room for a goat, you might even consider that, but remember that goats need to be milked morning and night, – and they eat bits of everything, including washing – so make sure you have help for that, or similar hobby, or you will just have another headache!

Virgos often make excellent secretaries and treasurers for clubs and societies. Our local society for astrology and related subjects boasts no less than three Virgos on the committee, running it beautifully, quietly and with amazing efficiency. Virgo has a secret attraction to the mystical and/or the mysterious, but you usually need to systematise it. Astrology offers a vehicle for this. Committees also give you that opportunity to be of service, but you will become a little waspish if taken for granted, and who can blame you?

Adult or spare-time education is also a Virgoan favourite: if you wish to expand your social scene or if you find time on your hands, you should find a course in which to enroll. This sign is often good at keeping up correspondence courses, also, so that is an option if getting out is difficult. In addition, Virgo often loves theatre and performing arts. There is an impish, mimicking quality to this sign and, added to the fine discrimination of the critic, much pleasure can be found in plays and the like – and you sometimes like to get directly involved. To the surprise of some, you may make fine actors and actresses. Virgo is interested in anything artistic and creative, and likes to bestow an informed opinion.

This sign is concerned with fitness and you often like to play sports. Team sports appeal, also cycling or jogging. Virgos are rarely fanatics, however, for their sense of proportion is too sound.

Holidays

Holidays are excellent for Virgo, and you should take them somewhere where work and other responsibilities do not intrude. Being a Mutable sign, Virgo often likes to travel and your organisational talent goes into overdrive, preparing and packing. Holidays should include a reasonable amount of activity – you can become fairly easily bored without it. Learning about history and other cultures will often appeal, and you may like to try out a few words of the local language. You should take care of what you eat and drink when abroad, for even if local food does not upset your system you may imagine it does, which is the same thing. Lots of trips, interesting conversation and things to see and comment upon are most stimulating and refreshing to Virgo.

■ YOUR STYLE

Before anyone runs away with the impression that Virgo is Ms or Mr Mouse, let me stress that this is most certainly not the case. This is an understated, elegant sign, but, as we have seen, a sensual one. Plenty of stars of stage and screen are Virgos – for instance, the glamorous Claudia Schiffer, and the sexy filmstar Keanu Reeves. Despite the passionate, seductive parts often played by the actress Sophia Loren, who is also a Virgo, from her books it is obvious that she approaches life with a certain detachment, much precision and refinement.

So, as a Virgo you will choose with taste and discrimination. Things will need to be useful, serviceable but also aesthetically pleasing. Yes, you will notice uneven hems, unmatched seams and hanging threads, and you will not want to pay good money for shoddy goods. Do try to restrain yourself from simply looking for trouble, because you will always find an imperfection somewhere, and it can be a waste of your valuable time. Colours should, for the most part, be muted and subtle, styles understated and superbly tailored and fabrics pleasant to the touch and of the highest quality. Comfort, too is important, and it will irritate you endlessly if what you wear pulls and puckers. Casual outfits are usually more practical, but many Virgos do look superb in formal wear. Finish an outfit off with accessories as stunning as they are subtle – a fine silk tie, an exquisitely crafted piece of jewellery.

Your living space needs to offer you the opportunity for order in whatever sphere you deem it necessary – for your books, paperwork, clothes or whatever. Of course, Virgos aren't always tidy, but few are fundamentally disorganised when you scratch below the surface. There should be room for some well-chosen pictures or *objets d'art*. Colours should be muted for most Virgos, as this sign can be disturbed by the gaudy, and fabric designs are small and detailed rather than bold. Naturally, you will need room for articles needed for crafts, if you enjoy those, and you will doubtless be particular as to their maintenance and storage. Virgo is often a technologically literate sign, and there may need to be room for computers, fax machines and a state-of-the-art hi-fi. Most Virgos do need a desk, for they usually have some activity or activities that can be comfortably undertaken only by sitting at a desk.

When you are choosing purchases for yourself or your home think simple, useful, smart, neat, subtle, elegant, poised, aesthetic, balanced, refined, quality, craftsmanship. You will rarely buy on impulse and should resist the temptation to waste time looking for flaws. Plan well, buy the best you can afford and enjoy it.

♍ Style and leisure ♍

■ PRACTICE AND CHANGE ■

- You need leisure to unwind, but you will rarely be at ease doing nothing. Make sure you have some reading or something else to do – knitting a scarf is better than knitting your brows!
- Hobbies, crafts and adult education are all to be recommended, and every Virgo with some spare time should consider these carefully.
- Virgo loves to improve her or himself in some way, and anything that makes you more well informed or skilful will give you endless pleasure.
- Fitness is important to Virgo. A sensible fitness programme is a good spare-time plan.
- When choosing purchases always go for quality, finish and craftsmanship. Remember that you enjoy what is sensually pleasing, to the touch and eye, and fine scents will give you special delight. You will always want the useful, but equally you appreciate the aesthetic – there is no need to sacrifice either.
- Look through your wardrobe. Is there anything that you bought because it seemed serviceable or attractive that you have never felt at ease wearing? Perhaps there is something exasperating about it, such as arms or legs of slightly unequal length or a collar that rubs the back of your neck. If it is too late to take it back to the shop then give it away. It isn't sensible to have it cluttering up your cupboard, and symbolically you will feel good at ejecting the unsatisfactory from your life.

Appendix 1

■ VIRGO COMBINED WITH MOON SIGN

Our 'birth sign' or 'star sign' refers to the sign of the zodiac occupied by the Sun when we were born. This is also called our 'Sun sign', and this book is concerned with Virgo as a Sun sign. However, as we saw in the Introduction, a horoscope means much more than the position of the Sun alone. All the other planets have to be taken into consideration by an astrologer. Of great importance is the position of the Moon.

The Moon completes a tour of the zodiac in about twenty-eight days, changing sign every two days or so. The Moon relates to our instincts, responses, reactions, habits, comfort zone and 'where we live' emotionally – and sometimes physically. It is very important in respect of our intuitional abilities and our capacity to feel part of our environment, but because what the Moon rules is usually non-verbal and non-rational it has been neglected. This has meant that our lives have become lop-sided. Learning to be friends with our instincts can lead to greater well-being and wholeness.

Consult the table on page 81 to find which sign the Moon was in, at the time of your birth. This, combined with your Sun sign is a valuable clue to deeper understanding.

♍ Appendix 1 ♍

Find your Moon number

Look up your month and day of birth. Then read across to find your personal Moon number. Now go to Chart 2, below.

January		February		March		April		May		June	
1,2	1	1,2	3	1,2	3	1,2	5	1,2	6	1,2	8
3,4	2	3,4	4	3,4	4	3,4	6	3,4	7	3,4	9
5,6	3	5,6	5	5,6	5	5,6	7	5,6	8	5,6,7	10
7,8	4	7,8	6	7,8	6	7,8	8	7,8	9	8,9	11
9,10	5	9,10,11	7	9,10	7	9,10,11	9	9,10	10	10,11,12	12
11,12	6	12,13	8	11,12	8	12,13	10	11,12,13	11	13,14	1
13,14	7	14,15	9	13,14	9	14,15,16	11	14,15,16	12	15,16,17	2
15,16,17	8	16,17,18	10	15,16,17	10	17,18	12	17,18	1	18,19	3
18,19	9	19,20	11	18,19	11	19,20,21	1	19,20	2	20,21	4
20,21	10	21,22,23	12	20,21,22	12	22,23	2	21,22,23	3	22,23	5
22,23,24	11	24,25	1	23,24,25	1	24,25	3	24,25	4	24,25	6
25,26	12	26,27,28	2	26,27	2	26,27,28	4	26,27	5	26,27	7
27,28,29	1	29	3	28,29	3	29,30	5	28,29	6	28,29,30	8
30,31	2			30,31	4			30,31	7		

July		August		September		October		November		December	
1,2	9	1	10	1,2	12	1,2	1	1,2,3	3	1,2	4
3,4	10	2,3	11	3,4	1	3,4	2	4,5	4	3,4	5
5,6,7	11	4,5,6	12	5,6,7	2	5,6	3	6,7	5	5,6	6
8,9	12	7,8	1	8,9	3	7,8,9	4	8,9	6	7,8,9	7
10,11,12	1	9,10	2	10,11	4	10,11	5	10,11	7	10,11	8
13,14	2	11,12,13	3	12,13	5	12,13	6	12,13	8	12,13	9
15,16	3	14,15	4	14,15	6	14,15	7	14,15	9	14,15	10
17,18	4	16,17	5	16,17	7	16,17	8	16,17,18	10	16,17	11
19,20	5	18,19	6	18,19	8	18,19	9	19,20	11	18,19,20	12
21,22,23	6	20,21	7	20,21,22	9	20,21	10	21,22,23	12	21,22	1
24,25	7	22,23	8	23,24	10	22,23,24	11	24,25	1	23,24,25	2
26,27	8	24,25	9	25,26,27	11	25,26	12	26,27,28	2	26,27	3
28,29	9	26,27,28	10	28,29	12	27,28,29	1	29,30	3	28,29	4
30,31	10	29,30	11	30	1	30,31	2			30,31	5
		31	12								

Find your Moon sign

Find your year of birth. Then read across to the column of your Moon number. Where they intersect shows your Moon sign.

Birth year					Moon number										
					1	2	3	4	5	6	7	8	9	10	11	12
1900	1919	1938	1957	1976	Leo	Can	Vir	Tau	Ari	Gem	Sco	Cap	Sag	Aqu	Lib	Pis
1901	1920	1939	1958	1977	Ari	Gem	Sco	Cap	Sag	Aqu	Lib	Pis	Leo	Can	Vir	Tau
1902	1921	1940	1959	1978	Aqu	Lib	Pis	Leo	Can	Vir	Tau	Ari	Gem	Sco	Cap	Sag
1903	1922	1941	1960	1979	Can	Vir	Tau	Ari	Gem	Sco	Cap	Sag	Aqu	Lib	Pis	Leo
1904	1923	1942	1961	1980	Gem	Sco	Cap	Sag	Aqu	Lib	Pis	Leo	Can	Vir	Tau	Ari
1905	1924	1943	1962	1981	Lib	Pis	Leo	Can	Vir	Tau	Ari	Gem	Sco	Cap	Sag	Aqu
1906	1925	1944	1963	1982	Vir	Tau	Ari	Gem	Sco	Cap	Sag	Aqu	Lib	Pis	Leo	Can
1907	1926	1945	1964	1983	Cap	Sag	Aqu	Lib	Pis	Leo	Can	Vir	Tau	Ari	Gem	Sco
1908	1927	1946	1965	1984	Pis	Leo	Can	Vir	Tau	Ari	Gem	Sco	Cap	Sag	Aqu	Lib
1909	1928	1947	1966	1985	Tau	Ari	Gem	Sco	Cap	Sag	Aqu	Lib	Pis	Leo	Can	Vir
1910	1929	1948	1967	1986	Sag	Aqu	Lib	Pis	Leo	Can	Vir	Tau	Ari	Gem	Sco	Cap
1911	1930	1949	1968	1987	Leo	Can	Vir	Tau	Ari	Gem	Sco	Cap	Sag	Aqu	Lib	Pis
1912	1931	1950	1969	1988	Ari	Gem	Sco	Cap	Sag	Aqu	Lib	Pis	Leo	Can	Vir	Tau
1913	1932	1951	1970	1989	Aqu	Lib	Pis	Leo	Can	Vir	Tau	Ari	Gem	Sco	Cap	Sag
1914	1933	1952	1971	1990	Can	Vir	Tau	Ari	Gem	Sco	Cap	Sag	Aqu	Lib	Pis	Leo
1915	1934	1953	1972	1991	Lib	Pis	Leo	Can	Vir	Tau	Ari	Gem	Sco	Cap	Sag	Aqu
1916	1935	1954	1973	1992	Vir	Tau	Ari	Gem	Sco	Cap	Sag	Aqu	Lib	Pis	Leo	Can
1917	1936	1955	1974	1993	Cap	Sag	Aqu	Lib	Pis	Leo	Can	Vir	Tau	Ari	Gem	Sco
1918	1937	1956	1975	1994	Pis	Leo	Can	Vir	Tau	Ari	Gem	Sco	Cap	Sag	Aqu	Lib

Ari | Tau | Gem | Can | Leo | Vir | Lib | Sco | Sag | Cap | Aqu | Pis

Virgo Sun / Virgo Moon

You are highly discriminating and particular in most spheres of your life. Although you may be quite capable of starting projects, it is unlikely that you do many things on impulse – all has to be weighed and sifted. You are probably a brilliant organiser and can be relied upon to deliver the goods efficiently and on time, from a simple essay to large-scale reorganisation of company procedures. To others it often seems that you are perfect, and they may fear your criticism. This is a laugh, really, for criticism is the thing that you most fear, and secretly you only feel lovable – or even barely likable – if you are quite without flaw. As this is an impossibility, you may unobtrusively worry yourself to death. Learn to give yourself a pat on the back now and then, and to love yourself for your glorious, untidy humanity. If you were 'perfect' you would be a very imperfect human.

Virgo Sun / Libra Moon

Attractive surroundings are important to you, and you probably value neatness, beauty – and peace. You do not like anything to interrupt the tranquillity of your days, but life isn't like that, and you may find yourself mending and making-do physically and emotionally. Sometimes you feel quite exhausted from trying to please everyone, and then it dawns on you that you are not pleasing yourself one iota. You may become irritable and sow discord without meaning to, in an effort to restore balance. Of course, this just makes matters worse. You *can* achieve balance and a near-perfect order if you will only listen to your own needs, as well as others. You are part of the equation. Peace and beauty depend also on a place for you in the scheme.

Virgo Sun / Scorpio Moon

You are never content with the surface of anything. Generally, you are an active, busy and efficient person. You can be counted upon to find the worm in any apple, the missing element in the equation and 'who dun it' in any mystery. It isn't easy to fool you, and you are as intuitive about people and their underlying motives as you are perceptive about practicalities. Quietly, you are a considerable force to be reckoned with. However, the trouble with burrowing around in basements can be that you bring the entire house down – and I'm not talking about applause! Be careful that you do not become destructive, cynical and suspicious. Remember also that the most important thing to 'get to the bottom of' can be yourself. Find out how to meet your needs without being devious with others. Have the courage to open out emotionally, not just sexually. Losing control isn't the end of the world – you may find a warmth and depth you hadn't imagined.

Virgo Sun / Sagittarius Moon

Just when you think you've got your whole life plotted in an orderly fashion, from birth to death, lo and behold you go and do something that upsets the apple cart again! Where do these impulses come from? How does your foot get in your mouth, your money leave your purse, and the back door get left open, despite all your efforts? The answer is that there is a part of you that appreciates there is more to life than order and predictability – a part of you that sees new meanings and far horizons, that loves to laugh and feel the wind in your hair, and that is far more interested in pushing back boundaries, conceptual or otherwise, than arranging them. Set yourself sensible limits that will enhance your internal freedom, rather than caging it. As you tend the hearth-flame always nurture the flames of the spirit in your soul – they are far from being mutually exclusive.

Virgo Sun / Capricorn Moon

Cool, calm and collected, you may make yourself so unobtrusive in the hustle and bustle that one day everyone wakes up to find – surprise, surprise – you have run off with first prize. You, on the other hand, knew all along where you were going. You are purposeful, orderly and practical – some call you a control-freak. Your standards are extremely high and you may deny yourself much in achieving them. People may find you a little cold and reserved. What they do not realise is that you probably feel insecure, inadequate and full of faults. Although you are not at war with yourself – you are fairly wholehearted in your perfectionism – you consistently strain to meet standards that you did not set, and that may be inappropriate for you. Find true strength in accepting your vulnerability. Review your standards to see if they really are worth the effort. Unbend a little – love your sensitivity, and others will warm to it.

Virgo Sun / Aquarius Moon

Approval is most important to you. You like to feel a useful part of a circle of friends and while you can't quite help picking things to pieces at times, it is important to you to feel valued, to contribute and to be generally friendly. At the same time you may fear true intimacy. Science may interest you – you may have a tendency to intellectualise or to become preoccupied with abstracts, and you can be clever, perceptive and individualistic. It is important that you identify who and what you are, and this may not be easy, for you tend to rationalise your emotions or try to 'rise above' them. Only when you have a true sense of your own uniqueness can you choose to be with people who will affirm this, and then you may find that you are quite inspired. This really is a fascinating world, and you are the most fascinating thing in it, so set yourself free.

Virgo Sun / Pisces Moon

It is deeply important to you to be useful and appreciated. You are able to merge with the needs of friends, but then rise to the occasion with practical help and sensible suggestions. You are rather torn between empathy and a more critical approach that wishes to see others help themselves also. You are very intuitive about what people are really like, but you may choose to forgive them anyway. You should take note of your dreams, for they may be revealing. Mostly what you need to learn to do is to look after yourself in the thorough way you usually devote to others. You can be critical, especially of yourself, and discontented. You may be so torn between the practical and the idealistic that you achieve little, or you may be able to draw on your rich imaginal world to create works that are quite exquisite, from soufflé to symphony. It is up to you to work to get the balance right.

Virgo Sun / Aries Moon

Sometimes you surprise yourself with your sheer cheek! You may see yourself as quiet, restrained and discriminating but others may sense in you a force to be reckoned with. If you see that something isn't 'up to scratch' you can be quite relentless about exposing flaws. You can achieve a great deal, for when the chips are down you will put everything into getting your way, or your point of view across. As you are generally well informed and down to earth, you are quite difficult to argue with. You may seem to get what you want, but deep inside you are often dissatisfied, yearning for 'something' and you may become critical and destructive rather than confront your true needs. However efficient and self-reliant you may be, there is only so much that anyone can do for themselves. Allow yourself to depend on others sometimes, it can be a heart-warming experience.

♍ VIRGO ♍

Virgo Sun / Taurus Moon

You love comfort and security and you are perfectly capable of achieving this for yourself. Deeply practical and realistic, you have nonetheless a great appreciation of the beautiful. You like everything to be of excellent quality and durability. Sometimes you may be impatient of the 'airy-fairy' – the tangible is more your territory. It can be very hard for you to let go of anything or anyone, and you may worry yourself to a frazzle thinking of ways to hang on. You may be prone to habits that you would do better to break. Because the material world seems so important to you, it may take a while for you to realise that true security can never be found in bricks and mortar or insurance policies. Take the time to discover the real you in all ways, from appropriate regimes and diets to true emotional needs and spirituality. Only in this way can you learn to loosen your grasp, to trust in the universe and feel secure in possession of your deep self.

Virgo Sun / Gemini Moon

You gather information like a bee gathers honey and you are probably very chatty and interested in what everyone else is doing. No, I didn't say 'nosey', though some might! What you want to do is understand and make connections, although you can use your inside knowledge a little waspishly at times. Generally, you are a clever person, efficient, sensible and orderly. You have a good grasp of basic concepts and can express yourself well, when necessary. You like to be able to explain everything, even your own feelings, and as these are not open to objective analysis you could become a little neurotic and erratic when under stress. Try to use your excellent powers of reasoning to come to terms with how you feel. Do not rationalise and analyse but find a place in your life for unruly emotions and learn to put into words how you really feel. You can be both deep and clever.

Virgo Sun / Cancer Moon

You are probably something of a 'worrier'. Although you go to considerable lengths to make sure you have done everything correctly you may still fear that some loose end is left to trip you. Probably you have sensible ideas about how to run your life from diets and bedtime to your bank account, but sometimes you just feel the urge for something more, and all the good resolutions go out of the window. You may relapse into dreams. However, you are a productive person, generally helpful, sympathetic and practical and you can make your dreams a reality. You can get into a routine and stick to it. You have homemaking talents and an intuitive knowledge of what people need which you can use to your own profit, specifically financially. Learn to make time in your schedule for some real self-gratification, and also to frame your feelings and needs into words. In this way you can make room for your inner child and be even more efficient at other times.

Virgo Sun / Leo Moon

Your inner pride drives you to the pinnacle of perfection, but it is doubtful whether you are ever satisfied with what you, or others have done. You try to earn love and approval through excellence. Your heart is warm and generous, but your discrimination moderates this and you may alternate between generosity and something closer to meanness. Although you seek attention, there is something in you which is hidden, and you may never feel really understood and accepted. For all your practicality, and indeed passion, you are not really well connected to your physical needs and may seek gratification in excessive ways which offend your own good taste. You are a true achiever, with ambition, energy and application – an earth-mover. You need to use that pragmatism to provide for yourself, rather than hoping others will give you satisfaction and joy. Love yourself – you deserve it!

Appendix 2

■ ZODIACAL COMPATIBILITY

To assess fully the compatibility of two people an astrologer needs to have the entire chart of each individual, and while Sun-sign factors will be noticeable, there is a legion of other important points to be taken into account. Venus and Mercury are always very close to the Sun, and while these are often in the Sun sign itself, so intensifying its effect, they may also fall in one of the signs lying on either side of your Sun sign. So, as a 'Virgo' you may have Venus and/or Mercury in Leo or Libra, and this will increase your empathy with these signs. In addition, the Moon and all the other planets including the Ascendant and Midheaven need to be taken into account. So if you have always been drawn to Aries people, maybe you have Moon or Ascendant in Aries.

In order to give a vivid character sketch, things have to be stated graphically. You should look for the dynamics at work, rather than be too literal about interpretation – for instance, you may find that you do not argue much with Sagittarius, but you may still be aware of some tension. It is up to the two of you whether a relationship works, for it can, if you are both committed. Part of achieving that is using the awareness you have to help, not necessarily as a reason for abandoning the relationship. There are always points of compatibility, and we are here to learn from each other.

On a scale of 1 (worst) to 4 (best), here is a table to assess instantly the superficial compatibility rating between Virgo and companions:

♍ Appendix 2 ♍

Virgo 3
Scorpio 4
Capricorn 4
Pisces 1
Taurus 4
Cancer 2

Libra 1
Sagittarius 2
Aquarius 3
Aries 3
Gemini 2
Leo 1

■ VIRGO COMPATIBILITIES

Virgo with Virgo

This relationship is unlikely to get off to a flying start, as you are both too reserved and cautious. Having commenced, however, you both at least have the satisfaction of knowing that you have come up to the high standards of the other! You may have extended, subdued arguments, where each of you puts your point of view with painstaking logic. These could degenerate into barbed comments from between gritted teeth – uttered softly, of course! On the plus side you will share a love of detail and a quiet sensuality. Let us hope you both like order in the same area, or someone could be clucking over paperwork while the other seethes in the larder.

As lovers The Earthy nature of Virgo ensures that you have the prospects of a good and satisfying sex life. Ms Virgo decides that here is a man who will not offend her good taste, yet can answer her physically. Mr Virgo feels this is a lady whom he can trust to *be* a lady, in most meanings of the word. This relationship may not be exciting, and you will need to be inventive to avoid tedium after a while. Be careful that you do not criticise each other – criticise the neighbours instead – or the icicles on the bedroom door will acquire lethal spikes!

As friends A quiet friendship is likely. You may find each other easy to be with, and you will be able to make plans and sort things out together. You may have great fun elegantly shredding all lesser mortals! Always be sure you do not criticise each other.

As business partners You are both practical, with an eye for detail, but the problem is you may both be nervous and indecisive at times. Being workaholics, call in someone else for some verve – a Leo?

Virgo with Libra

On the surface there may be many elements to attract these two signs. Libra has its own brand of perfectionism, and for elegance and attention to the outward forms of the relationship, Virgo can find no fault in Libra. As a couple your public image may be exemplary. Behind closed doors things may become somewhat bland, with each of you feeling something is 'missing' but not sure what.

As lovers Your sexual encounters are likely to be elegant and expert. Unless you have planets in Fire or Water signs, passion and emotion are likely to be lacking – however, neither of you may be too deeply troubled by this. Ms Virgo admires the smooth manners and sociability of Mr Libra, while Mr Virgo is charmed by the intelligence and chic of Ms Libra. Libra is rather more sociable and extravert than Virgo, and in time Virgo may feel their life is subsumed in social trivia. Libra may feel that Virgoan worry and nitpicking are disrupting the peace of the relationship and spoiling the social occasions – which are of more importance to Libra. In addition, Virgo may find Libra a little hedonistic at times. However, this relationship can work well, for you share excellent taste and discrimination.

As friends Libra is likely to value the opinions of Virgo, which may be very helpful from a conceptual level down to the nitty-gritty of choice of clothes and furniture, while Virgo finds Libran suavity soothing. You may enjoy outings to galleries, exhibitions or any such based on an interest you share. Libra can show Virgo how to loosen up a little, without offence to good taste – usually. Libra appreciates that things go smoother for Virgoan watchfulness.

As business partners Can be good. Libra excels at promotional matters, while Virgo plans the budget, and all else, behind the scenes.

Virgo with Scorpio

What you see isn't what you get in this duo. To the outsider there may seem to be little happening, but inside there's lots of smouldering. Both of these signs have a need to get beyond and below the superficial, although their style is very different, and they each have an intense need for privacy. Here there can be much mutual respect and gratification.

As lovers Scorpio brings out all the sensuality of Virgo, whose response is a delight to the Scorpion. Both of you are inventive lovers, and Virgo, for all its reputation, can be sexually very abandoned, when given security and approval – and these are supplied in good measure by Scorpio, for the most part. Ms Virgo admires the strength and uncompromising nature of Mr Scorpio, while Mr Virgo, although the intensity of Ms Scorpio may make him uneasy at first, finds he responds to the keen perceptions and deep feeling of the sign. Trouble can appear on the horizon if either of you feels criticised, for you are equally capable of vitriolic counter-attack, Virgo being the more subtle, but no less destructive. Scorpio may find Virgo's fussiness invasive, while Virgo may also feel invaded by Scorpionic ownership. You need to give each other space.

As friends Both of you like a mystery and you may share sleuthing activities of some sort. Generally, there is much that is easy and smooth between you, but a beautiful friendship could dissolve in the acid of criticism, so avoid it.

As business partners Pretty good. You are each provident with funds and generally circumspect. Scorpio can become fixated on goals while Virgo worries about systems, and so you may irritate each other at times. A Fire or Air sign would be an asset on the publicity side.

Virgo with Sagittarius

A zodiacal mismatch that occurs many times, because these signs have a fascination for each other. Sagittarius finds Virgoan ways of thinking most intriguing, while Virgo yearns to get the Archer 'sorted out'. Often these two signs end up finding each other irritating and impossible, but may find the ties quite hard to break, because there are so many advantages to the partnership. After all, who could keep the home fires burning for wayward Sagittarius better than Virgo? And who can expand the exquisite watercolour of Virgoan horizons into a wild and evocative van Gogh better than Sagittarius? This is unlikely to be a feather-bed relationship.

As lovers Sex is usually wonderful at first. The insecurities which Sagittarius is at such pains to hide (especially from themselves) are unobtrusively wiped away by the pragmatism of Virgo, while Virgo often finds Sagittarius plain exciting. Ms Virgo finds this man a challenge and wonders if she can be the one to make him settle down, while Mr Virgo finds this free-spirited lady very sexy – she stirs something within him that longs to see the light of day. Trouble can set in because Sagittarius cannot bear being caged and questioned, while Virgo waxes apoplectic at the messiness of Sagittarian life, from the physical – clothes in the four corners of the bedroom – to the lifestyle – money, schemes and dreams all over the place. Lots of tolerance and space between the two is necessary to preserve this relationship.

As friends Intellectual interests may draw you. Likely arguments about ideas, Virgo coming from the 'prove it, let me see it' angle while Sagittarius responds with 'what ifs' and the final cracker 'What's reality anyway?'

As business partners   Great, if you have separate niches, and Virgo is the money bags. Awful if you are forced together too closely.

Virgo with Capricorn

Two Earth signs, and here we have one of the classical zodiacal partnerships. You are both great planners and are unlikely to leave any aspect of your life together to chance. Capricorn can make Virgo feel very secure with reassuring pragmatism, although this relationship is often fairly low key.

As lovers   Sex between you can be very good, although it is unlikely to rise to the transcendent. There is a workaholic aspect to each of you, and you may put off lovemaking until you are both too tired. Although there is a strongly sensual aspect to each of you, you may fail really to light the other's fuse, unless there are shared planets in Water and/or Fire signs. Ms Virgo feels she can trust the rock-like Mr Capricorn, while Mr Virgo respects the efficiency of this lady, who makes him feel accepted. This partnership can endure to the Golden Anniversary and beyond, simply because it is generally acceptable, and because neither of these signs is tormented by divine discontent. Neither Capricorn nor Virgo is high on imagination, and so they may jog along very contentedly, quite unaware that there might be something better – and there is much to be said for this.

As friends   You will have much in common and may plan outings with military precision. Capricorn makes the plans while Virgo sorts out the details. Generally, you will enjoy doing things together, as opposed to speculating. Both of you can be moody – Capricorn has a Saturnian angst that descends periodically while Virgo becomes stressed out. You can support each other through these provided they do not coincide.

As business partners It is unlikely that you will end up in a mess, but neither of you is very good at speculating. You will need to be careful that you do not get in a rut.

Virgo with Aquarius

Some Aquarians, of the practical, restrained sort (Saturn, planet of discipline and restriction is the 'old' ruler of Aquarius before the discovery of quirky Uranus) can appeal to Virgos. The attraction is usually intellectual. Virgo finds Aquarius stimulating, but the more kooky members of the sign are too way out for Virgo, although they may be intriguing. These two can have some interesting discussions.

As lovers If you two are up in the small hours you are probably talking, talking, talking. The sheer variety and freshness of Aquarian perspectives keeps Virgo analysing and making sense of all the new data, while Aquarius 'gets off' on all the detail and common sense that Virgo produces. However, unless there are very strong contacts between other planets, sex is likely to be quite cool, after an initial experimental phase. Ms Virgo finds this free-thinker fascinating, while Mr Virgo admires the independence and intellectuality of this unusual lady. On the plus side, Virgo can bestow a healthy moderation on some Aquarian brainstorms, and Aquarius can certainly shake the smugness of Virgo. This relationship can endure because Aquarius is an idealist who likes to do the Right Thing, while Virgo doesn't like upsets. '*La grande passion*' is unlikely – but then, perhaps you don't need it?

As friends More eccentric Aquarians are out, but with others again there may be the intellectual spark. You may share scientific or 'fringe' interests, with Aquarius constructing a complex temple of concepts, to which Virgo then tries to give Earthy foundations. Between you, you can come up with some workable ideas.

As business partners Could be good. Aquarius has galvanic notions which Virgo will use, if they aren't too zany.

Virgo with Pisces

These zodiacal opposites have much to offer each other if they can succeed in pulling in the same direction. The mystical quality of Pisces has a fascination for Virgo, while Pisces may relax, feeling that at last someone can take care of all the boring details. However, Virgo can become overwrought sorting out the muddles, and then Pisces has to sort Virgo out. Pisces may become exasperated in the extreme by what they see as pointless nit-picking. You may wonder what on earth you are doing together, but if you can remember what attracted you, this partnership can work well.

As lovers The dreamy and infinitely responsive nature of Pisces frees something in Virgo, who may become very sensually active and expressive. These two can take each other to the heights. However, the depths also loom, for both of you can become neurotic. Virgos may feel they don't know where they are with Pisces, or where anything else is – or where Pisces is, for that matter. Pisces may find that what they thought was solid earth turns to shifting sand when Virgo gets the worries – so each can make the other insecure. However, at first Ms Virgo finds this gentle man irresistible, and Mr Virgo finds wells of emotions he never knew in the melting presence of Ms Pisces. You need to work at understanding and each give a little in the direction of the other.

As friends Without a sexual bond Pisces may find Virgo rubs them up the wrong way by constantly pointing out faults, and may wonder how Virgo can be so insensitive, while Virgo finds Pisces sloppy. You are both caring people and could work well together on charitable schemes.

As business partners You could worry the life out of each other. Pisces' dreams get shredded, Virgo's order sabotaged. You will need someone to mediate – and make decisions.

Virgo with Aries

You are intensely different, and because of this a Fire–Earth attraction may be powerful between you. Virgo loves to find things to complain about and Aries loves to do the complaining, so the two of you dining out may be every restaurateur's nightmare! In time the very things that attracted you may come to irritate each of you, so you need to remind yourself what these qualities are. With understanding you can be each other's complement.

As lovers At first sexual passion can run very high. Ms Virgo is stunned by this bold cavalier, or thawed by the smoulder of the quieter Aries. Mr Virgo finds the verve and enthusiasm of Ms Aries tantalising, even if he does feel a little uneasy about what she will do next! Virgo must be careful not to nit-pick or Aries may depart in a shower of sparks. If Aries can maintain independence and Virgo can feel reasonably secure, this relationship offers much.

As friends If Virgo approaches the subject tactfully, the sign has much to offer Aries in terms of directing his or her energy effectively, while Aries can really open life up for Virgo, helping them cut through all the shilly-shallying and finding much to enjoy. You just need to keep working on appreciation of the other's good points.

As business partners This can be an excellent combination, with Virgo to create order and Aries supplying lots of the ideas and initiative. Aries will usually happily act as the 'front man', while Virgo prefers to stay in the back room, checking details. Just as well, because Aries is unlikely to bother about them! Aries can hearten a worried Virgo, while the Ram greatly values having someone to do the filing. Virgo must not be taken for granted, however. Glittering prizes aren't always Virgo's style, but a warm glow of appreciation definitely is!

Virgo with Taurus

Two Earth signs together, and you have much in common. There is something about Taurean stability that can be very reassuring to skittish Virgo, although the Bull may be a touch unsubtle on occasion. Virgo may become irritated at Taurean stubbornness, but each of you appreciates the good sense of the other. Virgo values the provident approach of Taurus and doesn't mind too much clearing up after the lazy Bull.

As lovers The sexual side is likely to be smooth and pleasurable. You share a sensual, pragmatic approach, although the emotional dimension is likely to be lacking, and there may be little sparkle. Ms Virgo is impressed by the capability and down-to-earth attitude of Mr Taurus, while Mr Virgo feels at ease with this sensible, yet alluring female. Yes, you 'talk the same language' but it is the prose of the everyday, not the poetry of heart and soul. You need to work at keeping romance alive in your relationship. Yes, security and home comforts are important, but remember it is that extra 'something' that keeps love alive.

As friends All things considered, the two of you have what it takes for an abiding friendship. Taurus is quite imperturbable in the face of Virgoan fussing and wittering, and deeply values the attention to detail that makes all schemes run so smoothly. Virgo warms to the way the Bull has of enjoying life, feeling able to relax and open out.

As business partners This may be a very creative combination, for Virgo is inventive and resourceful, while Taurus may be extremely artistic. The practical approach that you share invites success. However, unless one or both of you has chart factors that suggest enterprise, your venture is unlikely to hit the heights.

Virgo with Gemini

Both these signs are ruled by the planet of communication and intellect, Mercury, and this indicates some common ground, although the style could hardly be more diverse. Gemini loves to play with ideas and Virgo, while being very resourceful, has the eternal impulse to bring things down to earth. You could irritate each other worse than a storm of gadflies and yet somehow be drawn together, always expecting to find common ground and yet arguing about every phrase. Nonetheless, this can be a stimulating partnership.

As lovers There is little about the Airy Gemini to light the kindling of slow-burning Virgo and so sex might remain theoretical, or simply marginal. On the other hand, with other planetary support, this could be a relationship of contrived, stylish and possibly kinky sensuality. Ms Virgo is entertained by the quick wit of Mr Gemini, while Mr Virgo respects the cleverness of Ms Gemini, although her unreliability makes him a little uneasy. If Gemini can learn not to be bored by Virgo leaning towards the practical and useful, and if Virgo can appreciate that an idea is valuable just as an idea, then these two can get along.

As friends Intellectual pursuits are likely to be the bonding factor, and you may enjoy discussing the relative merits of the Herbal

Healing class (Virgo) with Beginner's Russian (Gemini). Yes, you are each inventive and resourceful enough to find common ground, which is saying something!

As business partners Virgo finds Gemini unreliable, unpredictable and flippant, while Gemini chafes at Virgoan insistence on practicality. You are both highly strung and a crisis could phase you both. However, you have much to complement each other, and can be really good together. You will find it easier if there is a stable third party on board.

Virgo with Cancer

This can be a wonderful relationship for building domestic bliss, although Virgo may find Cancer somewhat messy! Cancer has a way of soothing all the Virgoan worries without being so unsubtle as to question and dissect them. Trouble can set in, however, if this is an especially touchy Virgo, bent on denying all vulnerability and bleaching the sink and scouring the oven as a cure-all for emotional pain. Virgo may hurt Cancer deeply by refusing help which they so patently need, and denying Cancer the practical security for which the sign yearns, and which Virgo can actually provide with comparative ease. Long silences may result in total emotional constipation in the relationship.

As lovers Sex can be blissful, after a slow start. Cancer unspokenly coaxes away all inhibitions, and Virgo is able to come into his or her own, finding a lustful indulgence never before imagined. Ms Virgo respects the caution of this man and warms to his solicitude. Mr Virgo finds Ms Cancer incredibly sexy yet somehow reassuringly accessible. Trouble can set in if Cancer tries to 'smother' Virgo, or if Virgo witholds. Also both of these signs are terribly touchy when it comes to criticism. Virgo needs to remember how it feels to be criticised, in order to understand Cancer's hurt withdrawal. This can be an enduring partnership, for neither relishes upheaval.

As friends   This can be a quiet but satisfying association of shared interests, such as crafts or collecting. Cancer can be very supportive to a harried Virgo, while Virgo can offer solid common sense to a worried Crab. Let's hope you don't get the worries at the same time!

As business partners   Okay, but a bit slow. Plug in some dynamism from elsewhere, or Cancer may get on Virgo's back.

Virgo with Leo

These signs may be very attracted but there needs to be some hard work at understanding and respect. Patient and dutiful Virgo may clean up after the Lion for years, until resentment manifests as stomach ulcers or vicious sniping. On the other hand, the larger-than-life and magnanimous personality of the Lion can be very expanding to Virgo. Virgo needs to make it clear from the word go that there are limits to the amount of dogsbodying Virgo is prepared to undertake, but by the same token must hold back from fussing at Leo, especially in public. Leo must show appreciation of Virgo's efforts.

As lovers   Sex is often very good initially between Fire and Earth signs. Virgo's reassuring pragmatism may ignite Leo to a steady flame. Virgo in turn feels good and responds more, after an initial tantalising reticence. Ms Virgo cannot help but admire the personality of Mr Leo, so different from her own, while Mr Virgo is dazzled by this glamourous, yet not-too-flighty female. Leo will try to ignore Virgoan nit-picking at first but may roar with rage if pushed too far, while Virgo may despair at Leonine extravagance. However, you are each a treasure to the other, and if you will but remember it, this relationship can endure.

As friends   Leo can really galvanise Virgo's life, sweeping Virgo into places and conceptual panoramas that had not been dreamed of –

or Virgo may simply decide that Leo is absurd, and Leo that Virgo is boring. If both of you are broad-minded and willing to experience and understand, you can get much from this friendship.

As business partners Virgo must hold the purse strings, for Leo has no idea about budgets – although Leonine ideas, very big ones, are voiced about everything else. Leo has flair and style, Virgo has planning and practically – a good mix, if you can get going together.

Appendix 3

■ TRADITIONAL ASSOCIATIONS AND TOTEM

Each sign of the zodiac is said to have an affinity with certain colours, plants, stones and other substances. Of course, we cannot be definite about this, for not only do sources vary regarding specific correspondences – we also have the rest of the astrological chart to bear in mind. Some people also believe that the whole concept of such associations is invalid. However, there certainly do seem to be some links between the character of each of the signs and the properties of certain substances. It is up to you to experiment and to see what works for you.

Anything that traditionally links with Virgo is liable to intensify Virgoan traits. So if you wish, for some reason, to be wild and careless, you should steer clear of the colour green and lavender essential oil. However, if you want to be your Virgoan, precise best, it may help to surround yourself with the right stimuli, especially on a down day. Here are some suggestions:

- **Colours** Most shades of green, brown, grey, pastels, sometimes crisp contrasts like white and black, navy blue, some yellows.
- **Flowers** Honeysuckle, lavender, lily, primrose.

- **Metal** No metal is specifically linked to Virgo, except perhaps Mercury, which is more appropriate to Gemini. Virgos may find silver harmonious.
- **Stones** Agate, aventurine.

Aromatherapy

Aromatherapy uses the healing power of essential oils both to prevent ill health and to maintain good health. Specific oils can sometimes be used to treat specific ailments. Essential oils are concentrated and powerful substances, and should be treated with respect. Buy from a reputable source. *Do not use any oil in pregnancy* until you have checked with a reputable source that it is okay (see 'Further Reading'). *Do not ingest oils* – they act through the subtle medium of smell, and are absorbed in massage. *Do not place undiluted on the skin.* For massage: Dilute in a carrier oil such as sweet almond or grapeseed, two drops of oil to one teaspoon of carrier. Use in an oil burner, six to ten drops at a time, to fragrance your living area.

Essential oils
- **Lavender** The most gentle of oils, lavender can be applied neat and is good for soothing stings, as an antidepressant, for easing muscular and joint pains, headache and sunburn.
- **Cypress** An astringent and antispasmodic, good for relieving coughs, period pains and controlling excessive perspiration.
- **Patchouli** Has anti-inflammatory properties, for ageing skin, sores and can be added to shampoo to combat greasy hair.
- **Peppermint** Good for relieving flatulence, combating nausea and as a refreshing footbath, when a few drops are added to a bowl of water.

Naturally, you are not restricted to oils ruled by your sign, for in many cases treatment by other oils will be beneficial, and you should consult a reputable source for advice if you have a particular problem. If a problem persists, consult your GP.

Your birth totem

According to the tradition of certain native North American tribes, each of the signs of the zodiac is known by a totem animal. The idea of the totem animal is useful, for animals are powerful, living symbols and they can do much to put us in touch with our own potentials. Knowing your totem animal is different from knowing your sign, for your sign is used to define and describe you – as we have been doing in this book – whereas your totem shows you a path of potential learning and growth.

The totem for Virgo is the Brown Bear, and you also have an affinity with Mouse and Turtle. You were born in the Harvesting Time. There is a difficulty here, for the North American lore is based on the seasonal cycle. Thus for those of you living in the Southern Hemisphere, it may be worth bearing in mind the totems of your opposite sign, Pisces. These are Wolf, Buffalo and possibly Frog, although Frog is for Water. The Pisces time is called Blustery Winds Time.

Brown Bear represents a great deal that is important to Virgo, for Bear is wise and resourceful, knowing instinctively where to find healing roots. These animals gestate their cubs through the darkness and privacy of winter, and they like to arrange their environment to suit their purposes. They are gentle when left undisturbed but can be vicious when cornered, and despite the fact they are unobtrusive, they have tremendous stamina. Because they hibernate, bears are linked to the realm of dreams, which may connect Virgo to more mystical territory and alternative reality.

Contacting your totem

You can use visualisation techniques to make contact with the energies of your birth totem. You will need to be very quiet, still and relaxed. Make sure you won't be disturbed. Have a picture of your totem before you, and perhaps burn one of the oils we have mentioned, in an oil burner, to intensify the atmosphere. When you are ready close your eyes and imagine that you are your totem animal – imagine how it feels, what it sees, smells, tastes, hears. What are its feelings, instincts and abilities? Keep this up for as long as you are comfortable, then come back to everyday awareness. Write down your experiences and eat or drink something, to ground you. This can be a wonderfully refreshing and mind-clearing exercise, and you may find it inspiring. Naturally, if you feel you have other totem animals – creatures with which you feel an affinity – you are welcome to visualise those. Look out for your totems in the wild – there may be a message for you.

Further reading and resources

Astrology for Lovers, Liz Greene, Unwin, 1986. The title may be misleading, for this is a serious, yet entertaining and wickedly accurate account of the signs. A table is included to help you find your Rising Sign. This book is highly recommended.

Teach Yourself Astrology, Jeff Mayo and Christine Ramsdale, Hodder & Stoughton, 1996. A classic textbook for both beginner and practising astrologer, giving a fresh insight to birth charts through a unique system of personality interpretation.

Love Signs for Beginners, Kristyna Arcarti, Hodder & Stoughton, 1995. A practical introduction to the astrology of romantic relationships, explaining the different roles played by each of the planets and focussing particularly on the position of the Moon at the time of birth.

Star Signs for Beginners, Kristyna Arcarti, Hodder & Stoughton, 1993. An analysis of each of the star signs – a handy, quick reference.

The Moon and You for Beginners, Teresa Moorey, Hodder & Stoughton, 1996. Discover how the phase of the Moon when you were born affects your personality. This book looks at the nine lunar types – how they live, love, work and play, and provides simple tables to enable you to find out your birth phase and which type you are.

The New Compleat Astrologer, Derek and Julia Parker, Mitchell Beazley, 1984. This is a complete introduction to astrology with instructions on chart calculation and planetary tables, as well as clear and interesting descriptions of planets and signs. Including history and reviewing present-day astrology, this is an extensive work, in glossy, hardback form, with colour illustrations.

The Knot of Time: Astrology and the Female Experience, Lindsay River and Sally Gillespie. For personal growth, from a gently feminine perspective, this book has much wisdom.

The Astrology of Self-discovery, Tracy Marks, CRCS Publications, 1985. This book is especially useful for Moon signs.

The Astrologer's Handbook, Francis Sakoian and Louis Acker, Penguin, 1984. This book explains chart calculation and takes the reader through the meanings of signs and planets, with extensive interpretations of planets in signs and houses. In addition, all the major aspects between planets and angles are interpreted individually. A very useful work.

Aromatherapy for Pregnancy and Childbirth, Margaret Fawcett RGN, RM, LLSA, Element, 1993.

The Aromatherapy Handbook, Daniel Ryman, C W Daniel, 1990.

Useful addresses

The Faculty of Astrological Studies

The claim of the Faculty to provide the 'finest and most comprehensive astrological tuition in the world' is well founded. Correspondence courses of a high calibre are offered, leading to the internationally recognised diploma. Evening classes, seminars and summer schools are taught, catering for the complete beginner to the most experienced astrologer. A list of trained consultants can be supplied on request, if you wish for a chart interpretation. For further details telephone (UK code) 0171 700 3556 (24-hour answering service); or fax 0171 700 6479. Alternatively, you can write, with SAE, to: Ref. T. Moorey, FAS., BM7470, London WC1N 3XX, UK.

Educational

California Institute of Integral Studies, 765 Ashbury St, San Francisco, CA 94117. Tel: (415) 753-6100

Kepler College of Astrological Arts and Sciences, 4518 University Way, NE, Suite 213, Seattle, WA 98105. Tel: (206) 633-4907

Robin Armstrong School of Astrology, Box 5265, Station 'A', Toronto, Ontario, M5W 1N5, Canada. Tel: (416) 923-7827

Vancouver Astrology School, Astraea Astrology, Suite 412, 2150 W Broadway, Vancouver, V6K 4L9, Canada. Tel: (604) 536-3880

The Southern Cross Academy of Astrology, PO Box 781147, Sandton, SA 2146 (South Africa) Tel: 11-468-1157; Fax: 11-468-1522

Periodicals

American Astrology Magazine, PO Box 140713, Staten Island, NY 10314-0713. e-mail: am.astrology@genie.gies,com

The Journal of the Seasons, PO Box 5266, Wellesley St, Auckland 1, New Zealand. Tel/fax: (0)9-410-8416

The Federation of Australian Astrologers Bulletin, PO Box 159, Stepney, SA 5069. Tel/fax: 8-331-3057

Aspects, PO Box 2968, Rivonia 2128, SA (South Africa).
Tel: 11-864-1436

Realta, The Journal of the Irish Astrological Association, 4 Quay Street, Galway, Ireland. Available from IAA, 193, Lwr Rathmines Rd, Dublin 6, Ireland.

Astrological Association, 396 Caledonian Road, London, N1 1DN. Tel: (UK code) 0171 700 3746; Fax: 0171 700 6479. Bi-monthly journal issued.